LET'S GO Map Guide
New York City

Jace Clayton
Editor

Lauren Feldman
Sarah Landreth
Leeore Schnairsohn
Researcher-Writers

St. Martin's Press �＆ New York

A NOTE TO OUR READERS

The information for this book is gathered by Let's Go researchers during the summer months. Each listing is derived from the assigned researcher's opinion based upon his or her visit at a particular time. The opinions are expressed in a candid and forthright manner. Other travelers might disagree. Those traveling at a different time may have different experiences since prices, dates, hours, and conditions are always subject to change. You are urged to check beforehand to avoid inconvenience and surprises. Travel always involves a certain degree of risk, especially in low-cost areas. When traveling, especially on a budget, you should always take particular care to ensure your safety.

HELPING LET'S GO

If you want to share your discoveries, suggestions, or corrections, please drop us a line. All suggestions are passed along to our researcher-writers. **Address mail to:**

> **Let's Go Map Guide: New York City**
> **67 Mount Auburn Street**
> **Cambridge, MA 02138**
> **USA**

Visit Let's Go at **http://www.letsgo.com,** or send email to:

> **fanmail@letsgo.com**

Distributed outside the USA and Canada by Macmillan.

Let's Go Map Guide: New York City.
Copyright©1998 by Let's Go, Inc. All rights reserved. Printed in Canada.
No part of this book may be used or reproduced in any manner whatsoever without written permission except in the case of brief quotations embodied in critical articles or reviews. For information, address St. Martin's Press, 175 Fifth Avenue, New York, NY 10010.

Format produced & designed by VanDam, Inc. Map design & cartography © 1998 by VanDam, Inc. All rights reserved.

ISBN: 0-312-18124-8

First edition
10 9 8 7 6 5 4 3 2 1

Let's Go Map Guide: New York City is written by Harvard-Radcliffe students employed by Let's Go Publications, 67 Mount Auburn Street, Cambridge, MA 02138, USA.

Let's Go® and the thumb logo are trademarks of Let's Go, Inc.

Contents

How to Use This Map Guide

Let's Go Map Guide: New York City is made up of two parts: a detailed fold-out map and a short pamphlet of information on getting around, getting by, and getting out in New York City. To integrate the two parts, there is a detailed street index at the end of the guide. Using the index, addresses and street names given in the listings can be placed in the context of the city at large. In addition, certain important sights are marked by numbered red squares on the maps. The numbers correspond to numbers on the List of Sights found on the last page of the guide. The List of Sights features page numbers for many of the sights, to help you quickly find related write-ups and reviews. In the text, the number of any sight marked on the map follows the name or phone number of the sight. Thus, you can easily find the location of a sight you've read about.

For more comprehensive coverage of the City, pick up a copy of *Let's Go: New York City* wherever fine books are sold.

Useful Phone Numbers

Emergency: 911
Airports: John F. Kennedy Airport 718-244-4444; **LaGuardia Airport** 718-533-3400; **Newark International Airport** 201-961-6000
 To find the toll-free number of any airline: 800-555-1212
American Automobile Association: 800-222-4357
American Express: 800-528-4800, 800-221-7282
Amtrak: 800-872-7245
Arts Hotline: 756-ARTS/2787
The Broadway Line: 563-2929
Concert Hotline (Rock/Pop): 249-8870
Consulates: Australian 408-8400; **British** 745-0202; **Canadian** 768-1600; **German** 308-8700; **Japanese** 371-8222; **South African** 213-4880
Directory Assistance (Telephone): 411
 Directory Assistance, other area codes: (area code)-555-1212
Fire: 628-2900 or 999-2222
Greyhound: 800-231-2222
Help Lines:
 AIDS Hotline: 800-TALK-HIV/825-5448
 Alcohol and Substance Abuse Information Line: 800-247-2042.
 Alcoholics Anonymous: 647-1680
 Consumer's Union: 914-378-2000
 Crime Victim's Hotline: 577-7777
 Crisis Counseling, Intervention, and Referral Service: 516-679-1111 (primarily for youths; includes the **Gay Peer Counseling Network**)
 Department of Consumer Affairs: 487-4398
 Gay and Lesbian Switchboard: 777-1800
 Helpline Telephone Services (Crisis Counseling): 532-2400
 Legal Aid Society: 577-3300
 Lesbian Switchboard: 741-2610
 MLM Talking Yellowbook: 718-921-1400
 New York Gay and Lesbian Anti-Violence Project: 807-0197
 Poison Control Center: 764-7667
 Runaway Hotline: 619-6884
 Samaritans (Suicide Prevention): 673-3000
 Sex Crimes Report Line, NYPD: 267-7273
Hospital: New York Hospital-Cornell Medical Center, Emergency room 726-5050
Lincoln Center: 875-5000
Macy's Concierge Service: 560-3827
Metro North: 800-METRO-INFO/638-7646 or 532-4900
Movie Phone: 777-FILM/3456
New York City Department for the Aging: 442-1000
New York City Taxi Commission: 221-TAXI/8294
New York City Transit Authority: 718-330-1234
NYC Department of Cultural Affairs Arts Hotline: 956-2787
NYC/ON STAGE Hotline: 768-1818
Police (non-emergencies): 374-5000, TDD 800-855-1155
Postal Answer Line (PAL): 330-4000
Tele-Charge: 239-6200
Television Networks: ABC 456-7777; **CBS** 975-3247; **NBC** 664-3055
Ticket Central: 279-4200
TKTS: 768-1818
Ticketmaster: 307-7171
Tourist Office (New York Convention and Visitors Bureau): 397-8222 or 484-1200

New York City

This rural America thing. It's a joke.

—Ed Koch

In 1626, in a particularly shrewd transaction, Peter Minuit bought Manhattan from the natives for 60 guilders, or just under 24 bucks. Today there are seven cities on earth with larger populations than New York City, but the Big Apple scoffs at them all. The City boasts a staggeringly diverse population, a spectacular skyline, towering financial power, and a dizzying range of cultural enterprises. Nowhere is the rhythm of urban life more pronounced than in New York. Cramped into tiny spaces, millions of people find themselves confronting each other every day in a metropolis that is just too big, too jumbled, and too exciting. "There is more poetry in a block of New York than in 20 daisied lanes," said O. Henry. And many New Yorkers agree with former Mayor Ed Koch, who said: "New York is not a problem. New York is a stroke of genius."

PRACTICAL INFORMATION

Tourist Office: New York Convention and Visitors Bureau, 2 Columbus Circle (800-692-8474 or 397-8222), 59th St. and Broadway. Subway: #1, 9, A, B, C, or D to 59th St.-Columbus Circle. Multilingual staff helps with directions, hotel listings, entertainment ideas, safety tips, and "insider" descriptions of neighborhoods. Helpful website at http://www.nycvisit.com. Open Mon.-Fri. 9am-6pm, Sat.-Sun. and holidays 10am-3pm.

Consulates: Australian, 636 Fifth Ave. (408-8400). **British,** 845 Third Ave. (745-0202). **Canadian,** 1251 Sixth Ave. (596-1600). **German,** 460 Park Ave. (308-8700). **Japanese,** 299 Park Ave. (371-8222). **South African,** 333 E. 38th St. (213-4880).

American Express: Multi-task agency providing tourists with traveler's checks, gift checks, cashing services, you name it. Branches in Manhattan include: **American Express Tower,** 200 Vesey St. (640-2000), near the World Financial Center (open Mon.-Fri. 8:30am-5:30pm); **Macy's Herald Square,** 151 W. 34th St. (695-8075), at Seventh Ave. inside Macy's (open Mon.-Sat. 10am-6pm); **420 Lexingoton Ave.** (687-3700), at 43rd St. (open Mon.-Fri 9am-5pm); **822 Lexington Ave.** (758-6510), near 63rd St. (open Mon.-Fri. 9am-6pm, Sat. 10am-4pm).

Taxis: Most people in Mahattan hail yellow (licensed) cabs on the street: $2 base, 30¢ each one-fifth mi. or every 75 seconds; passengers pay for all tolls. Don't forget to tip 15%. Ask for a receipt, which will have the taxi's ID number. This is necessary to trace lost articles or to make a complaint to the **Taxi Commission,** 221 W. 41st St. (221-8294).

Car Rental: All agencies have minimum age requirements and ask for deposits. Call in advance to reserve, especially near the weekend. **Nationwide,** 241 W. 40th St. (867-1234), between Seventh and Eighth Ave. Reputable nationwide chain. Mid-sized domestic sedan $59 per day, $289 per week, 150 mi. per day, 1000 per week. Open Mon.-Fri. 7:30am-6:30pm. Must be 23 with a major credit card.

Bicycle Rental: Central Park closes to cars, allowing bicycles to rule its roads Jan.-Oct. weekdays 10am-3pm and 7-10pm and from Fri. 7pm to Mon. 6am. **Pedal Pushers,** 1306 Second Ave. (288-5592), between 68th and 69th St. Rents 3-speeds for $4 per hr., $10 per day, $13 overnight; 10-speeds for $5 per hr., $14 per day, $19 overnight; mountain bikes for $6 per hr., $17 per day, $25 overnight. Overnight rentals require a $150 deposit on a major credit card, but regular rentals just need ID or a drivers license. Open daily 10am-6pm.

Library: New York Public Library, 11 W. 40th St. (661-7220, or 869-8089 for a recorded listing of exhibitions and events), entrance on Fifth Ave. at 42nd St. Non-lending central research library. Wide variety of exhibits on display. Open Tues.-Wed. 11am-7pm, Mon. and Thurs.-Sat. 10am-6pm. Exhibitions open Mon. and Thurs.-Sat. 10am-6pm, Tues.-Wed. 11am-6pm.

Taxes and Tipping: The prices quoted throughout *Let's Go Map Guide: New York City* are the amounts before sales tax has been added. Sales tax in New York is 8.25%, depending on the item. Hotel tax is 13.25%; there's also a $2 occupancy tax per single room per night and a $4 tax for suites. Remember that service is never included on a New York tab. Tip cab drivers and waiters about 15%; tip especially good waiters—or those who work at especially good restaurants—20% of the tab. Tip hairdressers 10% and bellhops around $1 per bag. Bartenders usually expect between 50¢ and $1 per drink.

Crisis Lines: Crime Victim's Hotline, 577-7777; 24hr. counseling and referrals. **Sex Crimes Report Line,** New York Police Dept., 267-7273; 24hr. information and referrals.

Hospital: New York Hospital-Cornell Medical Center, 520 E. 70th St., between York Ave. and FDR Dr. Emergency room, 726-5050. **Walk-in Medical Clinic,** 57 E. 34th St. (252-6000), between Park and Madison. Open Mon.-Fri. 8am-5pm, Sat. 10am-2pm. Affiliated with Beth Israel Hospital.

Emergency: 911.

Police: 374-5000, for non-urgent inquiries. 24hr.

Post Office: Central branch, 421 Eighth Ave. (330-2902), across from Madison Square Garden (open 24hr.). For General Delivery, mail to and use the entrance at 390 Ninth Ave. C.O.D.s, money orders, and passport applications are also processed at some branches. Call 1-800-725-2161 for a 24hr. info line which provides information on branch locations, hours, postal rates, and zip codes and addresses. **ZIP code:** 10001.

Area Codes: 212 (Manhattan); 718 (Brooklyn, Bronx, Queens, Staten Island).

GETTING THERE

Airplane

Three airports service the New York Metro Region. **John F. Kennedy Airport (JFK)** (718-244-4444), 12 mi. from midtown in southern Queens, is the largest, handling most international flights. **LaGuardia Airport** (718-533-3400), 6 mi. from midtown in northwestern Queens, is the smallest, offering domestic flights and air shuttles. **Newark International Airport** (201-961-6000), 12 mi. from midtown in Newark, NJ, offers both domestic and international flights at better budget fares (though getting to and from Newark can be expensive).

JFK to midtown Manhattan can easily be covered by public transportation. Catch a free brown and white JFK long-term parking lot bus from any airport terminal (every 15min.) to the **Howard Beach-JFK subway station,** where you can take the A train to the city (1hr.). Or you can take one of the city buses (Q10 or Q3; $1.50, exact change required) into Queens. The Q10 and Q3 connect with subway lines to Manhattan. Ask the driver where to get off, and make sure you know which subway line you want. Those willing to pay more can take the **Carey Airport Express** (718-632-0500), a private bus line that runs between JFK and Grand Central Station and the Port Authority Terminal (every 30min. 5am-1am, 1hr., $13). A taxi to Manhattan costs a flat fee of $30.

LaGuardia passengers can reach Manhattan two ways. If you have extra time and light luggage, you can take the MTA Q33 bus ($1.50 exact change or token) to the 74th St./Broadway/Roosevelt Ave./Jackson Hts. subway stop in Queens, and from there, transfer to the #7, E, F, G or R train into Manhattan ($1.50). Allow at least 90min. travel time. The second option, the Carey bus, runs to and from LaGuardia every 30min., with stops at Grand Central Station and the Port Authority Terminal (30min.-1hr., $9).

Newark Airport to Manhattan takes about as long as from JFK. **New Jersey Transit (NJTA)** (201-762-5100) runs an efficient bus (NJTA #351) between the airport and Port Authority every 15-30min. during the day, less often at night ($7). The **Olympia Trails Coach** (212-964-6233) travels between the airport and either Grand Central or the World Trade Center (every 20min. daily 5am-11pm; 25min.-1hr. depending on traffic; $10).

Bus

Greyhound (800-231-2222), grooves out of their major Northeastern hub, the **Port Authority Terminal** (435-7000), 41st. and Eighth Ave. (Subway: A, C, or E to 42nd St.-Port Authority). Be careful—with so many tourists, there are plenty of scam artists around. *This neighborhood can be especially sleazy at night.* To: Boston (4½hr., $27); Philadelphia (2hr., $14); Washington, D.C. (4½hr., $27); Montreal (8hr., $65). **East Coast Explorer,** 245 8th Ave. (718-694-9667 or 800-610-2680), offers budget full-day, scenic bus trips between New York, Boston, and Washington, D.C. All trips $35.

Train

Train service in New York runs primarily through two stations. On the East side, **Grand Central Station,** 42nd St. and Park Ave. (Subway: #4, 5, 6, 7, or S to 42nd St./Grand Central), handles **Metro-North** (532-4900 or 800-532-4900) commuter lines to Connecticut and New York suburbs. Longer routes run from the West Side's **Penn Station,** 33rd St. and 8th Ave. (Subway: #1, 2, 3, 9, A, C, or E to 34th St./Penn Station), as well as **Amtrak** (582-6875 or 800-872-7245), serving most major cities in the U.S., especially in the Northeast. (Washington, D.C., 4hr., $52). Also from Penn Station is the **Long Island Railroad (LIRR)** (718-217-5477), and **NJ Transit** to New Jersey (201-762-5100).

GETTING AROUND

For info on **Taxis** and **Biking,** see **Practical Information,** p. 1. For more info on New York city subways and buses, call **New York City Transit** at 718-330-1234 (daily 6am-9pm).

Subways

The fare for **Metropolitan Transit Authority (MTA)** subways and buses is a hefty $1.50; groups of four or more may find cabs cheaper for short rides. Once inside the subway you may transfer to any train without restrictions. Most buses have access ramps, but steep stairs make subway transit more difficult for disabled people. Operates 24hr. a day, 365 days a year. A free copy of the subway map is available at any subway token booth.

The city's **MetroCard** is now the dominant form of currency for public transit in New York—the card, containing a magnetic strip, can be used at all subway stations and on all public buses. Metro-Cards can also be used for subway-bus, bus-subway, and bus-bus transfers (transfer good for up to 2hr.). There are certain restrictions on bus-bus transfers (i.e. passengers on some north-south routes can only transfer to a bus going east-west). The card can be purchased in all subway stations and at many newsstands. At press time, several discount offers and unlimited ride passes were in the works. Find out the latest on the helpful MetroCard info line (638-7622).

Exercise caution riding the subways between 11pm and 7am, especially above E. 96th St. and W. 120th St. and outside Manhattan. Riding the subway at night is dangerous—don't ride alone.

■ The **Metropolitan Transit Authority (MTA)** also runs buses for $1.50 a ride. The MTA transfer system provides riders with a paper MetroCard valid for a free transfer within two hours. Just ask the driver for a transfer slip when you board and pay your fare. Ring when you want to get off. A yellow-painted curb indicates bus stops, but you're better off looking for the blue signpost or glass-walled shelter. Exact change or a subway token is required; drivers will not accept dollar bills.

FOOD

Financial District

Zigolini's, 66 Pearl St. (425-7171), at Coenties Alley. One of the few places in the area where indoor air-conditioned seating abounds, this authentically Italian restaurant serves huge and filling sandwiches ($5-7), as well as some great pasta dishes. Open Mon.-Fri. 7am-7pm.

Frank's Papaya, 192 Broadway (693-2763), at John St., very close to the World Trade Center. Excellent value, quick service. Hot dog 70¢. Breakfast (egg, ham, cheese, coffee) around $1.50. Open Mon.-Sat. 5:30am-10pm, Sun. 5:30am-5:30pm.

Little Italy

La Mela, 167 Mulberry St. (431-9493), between Broome and Grand St. Kitschy photos, postcards, and letters proclaiming changed lives plaster the walls. Eating "family style" means no menu, but the super-friendly staff will guide you to mouth-watering eats. The attitude here is hand-lettered on a sign outside—"Try you gonna love it." Pasta $6, entrees $12-15. Open daily noon-11pm.

Puglia Restaurant, 189 Hester St. (966-6006). Long tables mean fun and rowdiness. A favorite of New Yorkers and bold tourists. Pastas $7-10, entrees $8.75-18. Down a monstrous plate of mussels ($9.25), or try the *rigatoni ala vodka* ($9.75). Live Italian folk music nightly beginning at 7pm. Open Sun.-Thurs. noon-midnight, Fri.-Sat. noon-1am.

Caffè Roma, 385 Broome St. (226-8413), at Mulberry St. A good *caffè* gets better with time. A full-fledged saloon in the 1890s, Roma has kept its original styling intact. The pastries and coffee prove as refined as the setting. Try the neapolitan *cannoli* or the *baba au rhum* ($1.50 take out, $2.25 eat in). Potent espresso $1.60. Cappuccino, with a tiara of foamed milk, $2.40. Open daily 8am-midnight.

Chinatown

Excellent Dumpling House, 111 Lafayette St. (219-0212), just south of Canal St. Terrific vegetarian and meat dumplings fried, steamed, or boiled (around $4 for 8 pieces). Lunch specials (around $5.50) such as shredded pork with garlic sauce include choice of soup, fried rice, and a wonton. Served Mon.-Fri. 11am-3pm. Open daily 11am-9pm.

House of Vegetarian, 68 Mott St. (226-6572), between Canal and Bayard St. Faux chicken, faux beef, faux lamb, and faux fish comprise the huge menu; all meat is made from soy and wheat. Entrees $6-10. An ice-cold lotus seed or lychee drink ($2) hits the spot on hot summer days. Open daily 11am-11pm.

Bo Ky, 78-80 Bayard St. (406-2292), between Mott and Mulberry St. Tourists are a rarity in this excellent Vietnamese joint specializing in soups. It's hard to find anything on the menu that costs more than $3.75. Open daily 7am-9:30pm.

SoHo and TriBeCa

Bell Café, 310 Spring St. (334-2355), between Hudson and Greenwich. This low-key restaurant serves "ethno-healthy" cusine in an old bell factory. Always laid back, always healthy, always under $10. Off the beaten path, but well worth the journey. Enjoy free live music nightly. Outdoor seating. Open Sun.-Thurs. noon-2am, Fri.-Sat. noon-4am.

Prince St. Bar and Restaurant, 125 Prince St. (228-8130), at Wooster St. Artfully spare decor, beautiful people, and pretentious food (or is it beautiful food and pretentious people?). Archetypal SoHo. The gourmet (though affordable) French and Italian fare is joined by excellent Indonesian specialties ($6-11)—the stir-fry noodles with steamed vegetables and choice of sauce (peanut, garlic, or ginger) are great for dinner. Full bar with a selection of microbrews (pints $3-4). Open daily 11:30am-11pm.

Yaffa's Tea Room, 19 Harrison St. (274-9403), near Greenwich St. Wide selection of delicious sandwiches ($7.50) and entrees ($7-15) with used furniture decor. High tea ($15, reservations required) served daily 2-6pm. Open daily 8:30am-midnight. The attached bar/restaurant, at the corner of Greenwich St., is a little less subdued. Bar open nightly until 4am.

East Village, Lower East Side, and Alphabet City

Dojo Restaurant, 24 St. Mark's Pl. (674-9821), between Second and Third Ave. Unbeatable Dojo offers a variety of American and Japanese food that manages to be simultaneously healthy, delicious, and inexplicably inexpensive. Tasty soyburger, brown rice, and salad $3. Outdoor tables. Open Sun.-Thurs. 11am-1am, Fri.-Sat. 11am-2am. Another location at 14 W. 14th St. (505-8934).

Mama's Food Shop, 200 E. 3rd St. (777-4425), between Ave. A and B. Homecooking with a capital H. See laidback villagers settling in to heaping plates of fried chicken ($6) or salmon ($7), with $1 sides ranging from honey-glazed sweet potatoes to broccoli to couscous. Vegetarian dinner ($7) gives you any 3 sides. Scrape your leftovers and turn in your plate at the end of the meal, just like at good ole Mom's. Open Mon.-Sat. 11am-11pm.

Veselka, 144 Second Ave. (228-9682), at 9th St. Down-to-earth, soup-and-bread, Polish-Ukrainian joint. Enormous menu with 10 varieties of soups, as well as salads, blintzes, meats, and other Eastern European eats. Blintzes $3.50, soup $1.95 a cup (try the sumptuous chicken noodle). Combo special gets you soup, salad, stuffed cabbage, and melt-in-your-mouth *pirogi* ($8). Open 24hr.

Pink Pony Café, 174 Ludlow St., between E. Houston and Stanton St. Self-consciously hip cafe/ice cream parlor/bookshop catering to the Lower East Side artist set. A great place to study, read, or write over an espresso ($1.50). Try their lemon and ginger drink ($1.50). Performance space in back lends itself to stand-up comedy and screenings; call for schedule. Comfy chairs and couches. Open Sun.-Thurs. 10:30am-midnight, Fri.-Sat. 9:30am-4am.

Katz's Delicatessen, 205 E. Houston St. (254-2246), near Orchard St. A classic informal deli since 1888. The fake orgasm scene in *When Harry Met Sally* took place here. Have an overstuffed corned beef sandwich with a pickle (around $7). Open Sun.-Thurs. 8am-11pm, Fri.-Sat. 8am-midnight.

Greenwich Village

Cucina Stagionale, 275 Bleecker St. (924-2707), at Jones St. Unpretentious Italian dining in a pretty environment. Packed with locals on weekends—the lines reach the street at times. Sample the soft *calimari* in spicy red sauce ($6) or the pasta *putanesca* ($7). Pasta dishes $6-8; veal, chicken, and fish dishes $8-10. Open Sun.-Thurs. noon-midnight, Fri.-Sat. noon-1am.

Quantum Leap, 88 W. 3rd St. (677-8050), between Thompson and Sullivan St. Aggressively veggie restaurant with dishes such as BBQ Teriyaki Tofu ($8.50), soyburger delight ($5), spicy Szechuan beancurd ($8.95), and lunch specials. Don't worry, carnivores—it's all very tasty. Open Mon.-Thurs. 11:30am-11pm, Fri. 11:30am-midnight, Sat. 11am-midnight, Sun. 11am-10pm.

Olive Tree Café, 117 MacDougal St. (254-3480), north of Bleecker St. Middle Eastern food complemented by endless stimulation. If you get bored by the old movies on the wide screen, rent chess, backgammon, and Scrabble sets ($1). Falafel $2.75, chicken kebab platter with salad, rice pilaf, and vegetable $7.50. Open Sun.-Thurs. 11am-3am, Fri.-Sat. 11am-5am.

Elephant and Castle, 68 Greenwich Ave. (243-1400), near Seventh Ave. Their motto is *"j'adore les omelettes,"* and boy, are those omelettes adorable ($5.50-7.50). The strange omelette mixtures are unnerving, but worth a try. Open Mon.-Thurs. 8:30am-midnight, Fri. 8:30am-1am, Sat. 10am-1am, Sun. 10am-midnight.

Lower Midtown and Chelsea

Jai-ya, 396 Third Ave. (889-1330), at 28th St. Thai and other Asian food that the critics rave over, with three different degrees of spiciness, from mild to "help-me-I'm-on-fire." *Pad thai* $7.25. Lunch specials Mon.-Fri. 11:30am-3pm. Open daily Mon.-Fri. 11:30am-11:30pm, Sat. noon-11:30pm, Sun. 5pm-11:30pm.

Negril, 362 W. 23rd St. (807-6411), between 8th and 9th Ave. The Jamaican fare served here is light yet incredibly spicy. Jerk chicken ($7.50) comes with rice or grilled banana and steamed vegetables. Sandwiches $6.50-7.50, entrees $6.50-8.50, dinner $8-15. Spicy ginger beer $2. Festive Sunday brunch with live band 11am-4pm. Wheelchair accessible. Open Mon.-Sat. 11am-11pm, Sun. 11am-4pm and 5-10pm; Fri.-Sat. bar open til 4am.

Zen Palate, 34 E. Union Sq. (614-9291), across from the park. Fantastic Asian-inspired vegetarian cuisine, including soothing, healthy, and fabulously fresh treats like "shredded heaven" (assorted veggies and spring rolls with brown rice) for $8, stir fried rice fettuccini with mushrooms $7, or other concoctions on the brown rice/seaweed/kale and soy tip. Open Mon.-Sat. 11am-11pm, Sun. noon-10:30pm.

East Midtown

Dosanko, 423 Madison Ave. (688-8575), at E. 47th St. Very cheap, very fast, and very good Japanese food. Get the ramen ($5-7, depending on the toppings). Sit-down at their 217 E. 59th St. (752-3936) location, a few blocks up between Second and Third Ave. Open Mon.-Fri. 11:30am-10pm, Sat.-Sun. noon-8pm.

Maria Café, 973 Second Ave. (832-9053), between E. 51st and E. 52nd St. Pastries and pizzas made on the premises, and an incredible combo deal—$5.50 for pasta, salad, roll, and drink (daily 11am-3pm). Pita pizza $1.50. Open daily 8am-9pm.

Coldwaters, 988 Second Ave. (888-2122), between E. 51st and E. 52nd. Seafood ($6-11) served under nautical paraphernalia and stained glass lamps. Brunch is a bargain: two drinks (alcoholic or not), choice of entree, salad, and fries for $8 (daily 11am-4pm). Open daily 11am-3pm.

West Midtown

Afghan Cuisine Restaurant, 789 Ninth Ave. (664-0123 or 664-0125), between 52nd and 53rd St. This little cloister of things Afghani serves up superb, filling food. *Kebab* dishes (chicken, beef, or lamb marinated in fresh spices and broiled over wood charcoal, $7.50-8.50) and vegetarian platters ($6-7) with basmati rice, salad, and homemade bread. Open daily 11am-11pm.

Bali Nusa Indah, 651 Ninth Ave. (765-6500), between 45th and 46th St. Great Burmese food served in plentiful portions. The fried rice noodles with shrimp and chicken ($7.50) are a favorite, and the lunch specials, served with salad topped with a warm, spicy peanut dressing ($5.35, served daily 11:30am-4pm), are a bargain. Try the mango ice cream for dessert ($2.50). Open daily 11:30am-10:30pm.

Manganaros, 488 Ninth Ave. (563-5331 or 800-472-5264), between 37th and 38th St. This effortlessly classy Italian grocery and restaurant retains all the sights, sounds, smells, and flavors of pre-gentrification Hell's Kitchen. The staff will construct the sandwich of your dreams, or you can select from their vast menu ($3-12). Eggplant parmigiana ($5.25) is a local favorite, as are the pastas of the day ($7.50). Open Mon.-Fri. 8am-7pm, Sat. 8am-7pm.

Barking Dog Luncheonette, 1678 Third Ave. (831-1800), at 94th St. As the staff shirts command, "SIT—STAY!" and satisfy your hunger pangs with helpings fit for the biggest dog on the block. Breakfast special ($4.50), with two eggs, hash browns, and a choice of bacon or sausage biscuit. Burger platter ($6.50). Admire the dog-related paraphernalia adorning the walls during your meal. Open daily 8am-11pm.

Tang Tang Noodles and More, 1328 Third Ave. (249-2102), at 76th St. Lightning-quick service cuts through the crowds to deliver cheap, hot, tasty Chinese noodles and dumplings. Not one noodle dish over $5.75. Open Sun.-Thurs. 11am-11pm, Fri.-Sat. 11:30am-11:15pm.

Papaya King, 179 E. 86th St. (369-0648), off Third Ave. Hot dog hounds shouldn't miss the 100% beef "tastier than filet mignon" franks ($1.79) and fresh fruit drinks ($1.69) here. Open Mon.-Fri. 8am-midnight, Sat.-Sun. 8am-2am.

Upper West Side

H&H Bagels, 2239 Broadway (595-8000), at 80th St. Possibly the best bagels in Manhattan. Get a hot one (75¢). Open 24hr.

Cleopatra's Needle, 2485 Broadway (769-6969), between 92nd and 93rd St. Jazz and authentic Middle Eastern fare served up nightly to faithful locals. Take-out counter available to those on the go (Egyptian burrito under $4). Patrons have fun pronouncing exotic dishes like *Kibbeh sinaya* (baked ground lamb, $8) and *Imam Bayildi* (baked stuffed eggplant, $9). Open daily noon-11pm, dinner Sun.-Thurs. 5-11pm, Fri.-Sat. 5pm-midnight.

Café La Fortuna, 69 W. 71st St. (724-5846), at Columbus Ave. Delicious Italian pastries, coffees, and sandwiches served in a dark grotto of a cafe. A definite local favorite. Try the delicious iced cappuccino served with Italian chocolate ice ($3.75). Open Sun.-Thurs. noon-midnight, Fri.-Sat. noon-1:30am.

Harlem and Morningside Heights

Copeland's, 547 W. 145th St. (234-2357), between Broadway and Amsterdam Ave. Subway: #1 or 9 to 145th St. Excellent soul food without slick presentation. Smothered chicken $6.50; fried pork chop $7.20. Smorgasbord next door—cafeteria-style, but just as good. Open Tues.-Thurs. 4:30-11:30pm, Fri.-Sat. 4:30pm-midnight, Sun. 11am-9:30pm.

Massawa, 1239 Amsterdam Ave. (663-0505), at 121st St. Make sure your hands are spotless before heading here, a restaurant that specializes in cheap well-prepared Ethiopian cuisine—traditionally eaten by hand. The many vegetarian dishes ($5-6) are served with spongy *ingera* bread or rice. Between 11:30am and 3pm, they offer lovely lunch specials like lamb stew and collard-green/potato platters ($4-5.75). Open daily noon-midnight.

Tom's Restaurant, 2880 Broadway (864-6137), at 112th St. Suzanne Vega wrote a catchy tune about this diner, and Tom's is featured in most episodes of *Seinfeld*, but this eatery is mainly known for its luxurious milkshakes ($2.45). Greasy burgers for $3-5, dinner under $6.50. Open Mon.-Wed. 6am-1:30am and open continuously from Thurs. 6am to Sun. 1:30am.

Brooklyn

Oznaut's Dish, 79 Berry St. (718-599-6596). Subway: L to Bedford Ave., then walk west to Berry St. and head north. Scene: Antoni Gaudí meets ex-Manhattanite artists in funky Williamsburg and they build a restaurant in *kif*-dream Morocco. North African/American-eclectic fare, with plenty of cross-pollinated goodies like coconut Indian curry ($8) and lamb burger on peasant bread ($6.50). Iron Goddess of Mercy is one of 40 teas. Open Tues.-Sun. 6am-midnight.

Tom's Restaurant, 782 Washington Ave. (718-636-9738), at Sterling Pl. Subway: #2 or 3 to Brooklyn Museum. Walk a half-block east to Washington St. and then 1½ blocks north. Old-time luncheonette complete with a soda fountain and 50s-style hyper-friendly service. Two eggs with fries or grits, toast, and coffee or tea $2. Breakfast served all day. Open Mon.-Sat. 6:30am-4pm.

Nathan's (718-946-2206), Surf and Stillwell Ave., on Coney Island. Subway: B, D, F, or N to Coney Island. Across from the subway. Nathan's crunchy dogs have become nationally famous since their debut in 1922, and are now sold in franchises and supermarkets. A classic frank at the original Nathan's sells for $1.85. Try the fries, too. Open Sun.-Thurs. 8am-4am, Fri.-Sat. 8am-5am.

Queens

Pastrami King, 124-24 Queens Blvd. (718-263-1717), near 82nd Ave., in Kew Gardens. Subway: E or F to Union Tpke./Kew Gardens. Exit station following sign that says "Courthouse" and "Q10 bus;" then go left following the sign to the north side of Queens Blvd.; it's 2 blocks ahead and across the street. Everything here, from the meats to the slaw to the pickles, is made on the premises. Take on a sprawling, 3-inch-thick pastrami on rye for $9. Open Tues.-Sun. 9:30am-11pm.

Uncle George's, 33-19 Broadway, Astoria (718-626-0593), at 33rd St. Subway: N to Broadway, then 2 blocks east; or G or R to Steinway St., then 4 blocks west. This popular Greek restaurant serves inexpensive and hearty Greek delicacies around the clock. All entrees are under $12; try the roast leg of lamb with potatoes ($8). Cash only. Open 24hr.

East Lake, 42-33 Main St. (718-539-8532), at Franklin St., Flushing. Subway: #7 to Main St. Flushing. Four blocks down Main St., on the left. Converted 50s diner serves up kitsch and 148 Chinese dishes (photos illustrate the most complicated). Entrees are uniformly enormous ($8-16). Open daily 9am-2am.

The Bronx

Mario's, 2342 Arthur Ave. (718-584-1188), near 186th St. A neighborhood fixture for five generations, Mario's appears in the pages of Puzo's *Godfather*. Celebrities still pass through, among them the starting lineups for the Yankees and Giants. Try *spiedini alla romana,* a deep-fried sandwich made with anchovy sauce and mozzarella ($8). Notorious for pizza, too. Traditional pasta $9.50-11.50, *antipasti* $5.50. Open Sun. and Tues.-Thurs. noon-10:30pm, Fri.-Sat. noon-midnight.

Dominick's, 2335 Arthur Ave. (718-733-2807), near 186th St. There's no menu at this small, family-style Italian eatery—locals will be happy to give advice. Linguine with mussels and marinara ($7) and veal *francese* ($12) are all time-honored house specials. Arrive before 6pm or after 9pm, or expect a 20min. wait. Open Mon. and Wed.-Sat. noon-10pm, Fri. noon-11pm, Sun. 1-9pm.

De Lillo Pastry Shop, 606 E. 187 St. (718-367-8198), near Arthur Ave. Although this small shop is often crowded, it's worth your while to sit here and sample the excellent baked goods ($1-2) along with a cappuccino ($1.75) or espresso ($1.25). Open Mon.-Fri. 8am-7pm, Sat.-Sun. 8am-8pm.

ENTERTAINMENT AND NIGHTLIFE

Publications with especially noteworthy sections on nightlife include *The Village Voice, Time Out: New York, New York* magazine, and the Sunday edition of *The New York Times.* An **entertainment hotline** (360-3456; 24hr.) covers entertainment in the parks. For theater, music, and art info call **765-ARTS**/2787.

Bars

Beauty Bar, 231 E. 14 St. (539-1389), between 2nd and 3rd Ave. This bar used to be a hair parlor—and they haven't touched a thing. Patrons now settle here to quaff $3.50-4.50 beers and take in the funky decor. Crowded with East Village natives any night of the week. Open Sun.-Thurs. 5pm-4am, Fri.-Sat. 7pm-4am.

The Slaughtered Lamb Pub, 182 W. 4th St. (800-627-5262), at Jones St. A faux-sinister English pub dedicated to the werewolf, from lore to Jackson's *Thriller*. More than 150 types of beer ($5-20 per bottle), yards of ale, and darts and billiards downstairs in the "dungeon."Open Sun.-Wed. noon-3am, Thurs.-Sat. noon-4am.

Spy, 101 Greene St. (343-9000), near Spring St. A cross between an 18th-century salon and an MTV video with reasonably priced beers ($4-5), and an incomparable view of the legendary SoHo fashion/art/film crowd. Grab a couch early. Open daily 5pm-4am.

Max Fish, 178 Ludlow St. (529-3959), at Houston St. in the Lower East Side. The crowd is hip, if a bit pretentious, and the all-CD jukebox is easily the best in town: The Fugees, The Stooges, and Superchunk. Beer $2.50. Open daily 5:30pm-4am.

McSorley's Old Ale House, 15 E. 7th St. (473-9148), at Third Ave. Among the oldest bars in the city, McSorley's has seen Abe Lincoln, the Roosevelts, and John Kennedy since opening in 1854. Somewhat scruffier crowd on Fri. and Sat. nights. Great selection of beers. Open Mon.-Sat. 11am-1am, Sun. 1pm-1am.

Manny's Car Wash, 1558 Third Ave. (369-2583), between 87th and 88th Ave. Done up like a drive-thru car wash on Muddy Waters Drive, this place hosts some smokin' blues. All-you-can-drink (4-9pm) for $6. Women drink free Mon. night. Happy hour Wed.-Sat. 5-8pm. Open daily 5pm-3:30am.

Jazz

The **JVC Jazz Festival** (501-1390) blows into the city in June. All-star performances have included Ray Charles and Mel Torme. Tickets go on sale in early May. Summer's **Texaco Jazz Festival** brings in local talent as well as giants on the forefront of innovation. Concerts take place throughout the city but are centered at TriBeCa's **Knitting Factory.** Call 219-3500 in the spring for more info.

Apollo Theatre (#39; B12), 253 W. 125th St. (749-5838, box office 864-0372), between Frederick Douglass Blvd. and Adam Clayton Powell Blvd. Subway: #1, 2, 3, or 9 to 125th St. Historic Harlem landmark has heard Duke Ellington, Count Basie, Ella Fitzgerald, and Billie Holliday. Legendary Amateur Night (where the audience boos bad acts off the stage) $10-18.

Blue Note, 131 W. 3rd St. (475-8592), near MacDougal St. Subway: A, B, C, D, E, F, or Q to Washington Sq. The legendary jazz club is now a commercialized concert space with crowded tables and a sedate audience. Cover for top performers $20 and up. Sets Sun.-Thurs. 9 and 11:30pm, Fri.-Sat. 9, 11:30pm, and 1:30am.

Village Vanguard, 178 Seventh Ave. (255-4037), between W. 11th St. and Greenwich. Subway: #1, 2, 3, or 9 to 14th St. A windowless, wedge-shaped cavern, as old and hip as jazz itself. The walls are thick with memories of Leadbelly, Miles Davis, and Sonny Rollins. Cover $15 plus $10 min., Fri.-Sat. $15 plus $8 min. Sets Sun.-Thurs. 9:30 and 11:30pm, Fri.-Sat. 9:30, 11:30pm, and 1am.

Rock and Pop Clubs

New York City has a long history of producing bands on the vanguard of pop music and performance, from the Velvet Underground to the Wu-Tang Clan to Ani DeFranco to DJ Spooky. Also, keep in mind that virtually every band that tours the U.S. comes to New York City. Call the **Concert Hotline** (249-8870), or check out the exhaustive and indispensable club listings in *The Village Voice* to find out who's in town.

In addition to the venues listed below, the **Bottom Line** (228-7880), **Maxwell's** (201-798-4064), the **Cooler** (229-0785), and **The Bitter End** (673-7030) are all fine clubs for live music of all varieties.

CBGB/OMFUG (CBGB's), 315 Bowery (982-4052), at Bleecker St. Subway: #6 to Bleecker St. The initials stand for "country, blue-grass, blues, and other music for uplifting gourmandizers," but everyone knows that since 1976 this club has been all about punk rock. Blondie and the Talking Heads got their starts here, and the club continues to be *the* place to see great rock. Shows nightly at around 8pm. Cover $5-10.

Knitting Factory, 74 Leonard St. (219-3055), between Broadway and Church St. Subway: #1, 2, 3, 6, 9, A, C, or E to Canal. Walk up Broadway to Leonard St. Free-thinking musicians anticipate the Apocalypse with a wide range of edge-piercing performances complemented by great acoustics. Several shows nightly. Cover (usually $10) for the back room/performance space only; entry to the cozy bar up front is always free.

Mercury Lounge, 217 E. Houston St. (260-4700), at Ave. A. Subway: F to Second Ave.-E. Houston St. The Mercury has attracted an amazing number of big-name acts running the gamut from folk to pop to noise. Music nightly; cover usually $5-15.

Dance Clubs

Tunnel, 220 Twelfth Ave. (695-7292), near 28th St. Subway: C or E to 23rd St. Immense club; 3 floors packed with 2 dance floors, lounges, glass-walled live shows, and a skateboarding cage. Enough room for a multitude of parties in this labyrinthine club. Cover $20. Open Fri.-Sat.; Sat. nights are gay.

Webster Hall, 125 E. 11th St. (353-1600), between Third and Fourth Ave. Subway: #4, 5, 6, L, N, or R to Union Sq.-14th St. Walk 3 blocks south and a block east. Popular club offers dancing, a reggae room, and a coffee shop. "Psychedelic Thursdays" often feature live bands. Cover $15-20. Open Wed.-Sat. 10pm-4am.

Coney Island High, 15 St. Mark's Place (674-7959). Subway: N or R to 8th St. or #6 to Astor Place. High-energy venue offering several different themes—it may not be Coney Island but it is a ride. Mon. nights, **Konkrete Jungle** packs in the hardsteppin' junglists with drum 'n' bass and trip-hop downstairs; Sun. nights the top floor zooms with **Fast Times,** an 80s new wave party. Cover ranges from free to $10, depending on the night.

Nell's, 246 W. 14th St. (675-1567), between Seventh and Eighth Ave. Subway: #1, 2, 3, or 9 to 14th St. A legendary hot spot in slight decline; faithful admirers hang on for jazzy, soulful music upstairs and phat beats below. Diverse crowd. Cover Mon.-Wed. $7; Thurs. and Sun. $10; Fri.-Sat. $15. Open daily 10pm-4am.

Gay and Lesbian Clubs

Clit Club, 432 W. 14th St. (529-3300), at Washington St. Subway: A, C, or E to 14th St. Fri. nights in the Bar Room. The grandmother of NYC dyke clubs, the Clit consistently draws one of the younger and more diverse crowds around. This is *the* place to be for young, beautiful, queer grrls. Women only. Cover $3 before 11pm, $7 after 11pm. Doors open at 9:30pm. Tues. nights at the same space becomes **Jackie 60,** (366-5680). Drag queens work it while the crowd eggs them on to even more fabulous feats of glamour. Frequent theme nights with performances at around 11:30pm. Cover $5 before 11:30, $10 after. Doors open at 10pm.

Uncle Charlie's, 56 Greenwich Ave. (255-8787), at Perry St. Subway: #1 or 9 to Christopher St. Biggest and best-known gay club in the city. Guppies galore. Women welcome, but few come. Open daily 3pm-4am.

The Pyramid, 101 Ave. A (420-1590), at 6th St. Subway: #6 to Astor Pl. Also known by its street address, this dance club mixes gay, lesbian, and straight folks. Vibrant drag scene. Fri. is straight night. Cover $5-10. Open daily 9pm-4am.

Miscellaneous Hipster Hangouts

Soundlab (726-1724). Cultural Alchemy in the form of a nomadic happening. Expect a smart, funky, racially mixed crowd absorbing smart, funky, radically mixed sound. Call the info line to find where the next Lab goes down; past locales include the base of the Brooklyn Bridge, the 15th floor of a Financial District skyscraper, and outdoors in a Chinatown park.

Nuyorican Poets Café, 236 E. 3rd St. (505-8183), between Ave. B and Ave. C. Subway: F to Second Ave. Walk 3 blocks north and 3 blocks east. New York's leading venue for poetry slams and spoken word performances. Cover $5-10.

Collective Unconscious, 145 Ludlow St. (254-5277), south of Houston St. Plays, rock shows, and other performances (cover usually $5-7). Open-mike night Wed. at 9pm. Ongoing serial play on Sat. at 8pm ($5). Bring your own refreshments.

Theater

Call the **NYC/ON STAGE** hotline at 768-1818 or **Ticket Central** between 1 and 8pm at 279-4200 for information on shows and ticket availability. *Listings,* a weekly guide to entertainment in Manhattan ($1), has listings of Broadway, Off-Broadway, and Off-Off-Broadway shows. Broadway tickets cost $50 or more each when purchased through regular channels. **TKTS** sells tickets at 25-75% discount for many Broadway shows on the same day of the performance from a booth in the middle of Duffy Square (the northern part of Times Square, at 47th and Broadway; 768-1818 for recorded info). There is a $2.50 service charge per ticket; only cash or traveler's checks are accepted. (Tickets sold Mon.-Sat. 3-8pm for evening performances, Wed. and Sat. 10am-2pm for matinees, Sun. noon-8pm for matinees and evening performances.) **Ticketmaster** (307-7171; 24hr.) deals in everything from Broadway shows to mud-truck races; they charge at least $2 more than other outlets, but they take most major credit cards.

Joseph Papp Public Theater (#26; C4), 425 Lafayette St. (539-8750). For years, this theater was inextricably linked with its namesake founder, one of the city's leading producers. Tickets $15-35. About ¼ of the seats are sold for $10 on the day of performance (starting at 6pm for evening shows and 1pm for matinees).

La Mama, 74a E. 4th St (254-6468) is part of the great New York performance art tradition; an amalgam of stand-up comedy, political commentary, and theatrical monologue. This is the place that helped Sam Shepard get his start.

Provincetown Playhouse, 133 MacDougal St. A huge figure in Village history. Some of the most noteworthy Villagers are associated with this playhouse, including Eugene O'Neill and Edna St. Vincent Millay. Starting out in 1915 as a group producing plays on a porch in Cape Cod, the Provincetown put on many controversial, avant-garde acts in the 1920s such as Dada drama and the puzzling works of e.e. cummings.

Opera and Dance

Lincoln Center (#36; B8), on Columbus Ave. (875-5000), between 62nd and 66th St., is New York's one-stop shopping mall for high-culture consumers. There's usually opera or dance at one of its venues, which include Avery Fisher Hall, the New York State Theater, the Metropolitan Opera House, the Library and Museum of Performing Arts, the Vivian Beaumont Theater, The Walter Reade Theater, and the Juilliard School of Music. Write Lincoln Center Plaza, NYC 10023, or drop by its Performing Arts Library for a full schedule and a press kit as long as the *Ring cycle.* Also, **music schools** often stage opera performances; see Music for further details.

Opera

Metropolitan Opera Company, (#36; B8; 362-6000). Opera's premier outfit plays on a Lincoln Center stage—the Met. Regular tickets run as high as $160—go for the upper balcony (around $22; the cheapest seats have an obstructed view) unless you're prone to vertigo. You can stand in the orchestra ($14) along with the opera freakazoids who've brought along the score, or all the way back in the Family Circle ($15). Regular season runs Sept.-

April Mon.-Sat.; box office open Mon.-Sat. 10am-8pm, Sun. noon-6pm. In the summer, watch for free concerts in city parks (call the ticket line at 362-6000).

New York City Opera, (#36; B8; 870-5570) perpendicular to the Met. "City" came into its own under the direction of Christopher Keene. The company has a split season (Sept.-Nov. and March-April) and keeps ticket prices low year-round ($20-80). For $10 rush tickets, call the night before and wait in line the morning of.

New York Grand Opera, (360-2777) at Central Park Summerstage. Look for their free performances every Wed. night in July.

Amato Opera Company, 319 Bowery (228-8200; Sept.-May). Check the papers for their performances of the old operas.

Dance

New York City Ballet, (#36; B8; 870-5570). The late, great George Balanchine's dance company is one of the country's oldest and most famous, and dances at Lincoln Center's New York State Theater. Decent tickets for the *Nutcracker* in December sell out almost immediately. (Performances Nov.-Feb. and April-June. Tickets $12-65, standing room $12.)

The American Ballet Theater (#36; B8; 477-3030, box office 362-6000) dances at the Met every May and June (tickets $16-95).

The Alvin Ailey American Dance Theater (767-0940) bases its repertoire of modern dance on jazz, spirituals, and contemporary music. Often on the road, it always performs at the **City Center** in December. Tickets ($15-40) can be difficult to obtain. Call the box office (581-7907), weeks in advance.

Joyce Theater, 175 Eighth Ave. (242-0800), between 18th and 19th St. Experimental dance troupes (tickets from $15-40).

Martha Graham Dance Co., 316 E. 63rd St. (832-9166). The founder of modern dance and the most famous experimental company. Original Graham pieces performed during the Company's October New York season (tickets $15-40).

Merce Cunningham Dance Company (255-8240), of John Cage fame. Stages a 1-2 week season of performances each year at the City Center (131 W. 55th St.; 581-1212).

Classical Music

Begin with the ample listings in *Time Out: New York, The New York Times, The New Yorker,* or *New York* magazine. Remember that many events, such as outdoor music, are seasonal.

Lincoln Center (#36, B8), Columbus Ave. (546-2656), between 62nd and 66th St. The halls here have a wide, year-round selection of concerts. The **Great Performers Series,** featuring famous and foreign musicians, packs the Avery Fisher and Alice Tully Halls and the Walter Reade Theater, from October until May (call 721-6500; tickets from $11). **Avery Fisher Hall** (#36; B8; 875-5030; wheelchair accessible), paints the town ecstatic with its annual **Mostly Mozart Festival.** Arrive early; there are usually pre-concert recitals beginning 1hr. before the main concert and free to ticketholders. Festival runs July-Aug., tickets to individual events $12-30.

The New York Philharmonic (336, B8; 875-5656), begins its regular season at Avery Fisher Hall in mid-Sept. Tickets $10-60; call 721-6500 Mon.-Sat. 10am-8pm, Sun. noon-8pm. Students and seniors can sometimes get **$5 tickets;** call for availability (Tues.-Thurs. only). Anyone can get $10 tickets for certain **morning rehearsals;** again, call ahead. In late June for a few weeks, Kurt Masur and friends lead the posse at **free concerts** (875-5709) on the Great Lawn in Central Park, in Prospect Park in Brooklyn, in Van Cortland Park in the Bronx, and elsewhere. Free outdoor events at Lincoln Center occur all summer; call 875-5400.

Carnegie Hall (#40; B7), Seventh Ave. at 57th St. (247-7800), is still the favorite coming-out locale of musical debutantes. Box office open Mon.-Sat. 11am-6pm, Sun. noon-6pm; tickets $10-60.

92nd Street Y, 1395 Lexington Ave. (996-1100). Subway: #6 to 96th St. Cultural life on the Upper East Side revolves around the 92nd Street Y. The Y's Kaufmann Concert Hall seats only 916 people and offers an intimate setting with flawless acoustics and the oaken ambience of a Viennese salon. The Y is the home of the **New York Chamber Symphony** under the fiery direction of Gerard Schwarz. In addition, the Y plays host to a panoply of world-class visiting musicians. Concerts $15-40.

Music schools: Local schools give cheap New York music culture. Except for opera and ballet productions ($5-12), concerts at the following schools are free and frequent: The **Juilliard School of Music,** Lincoln Center (#36; B8; 769-7406), the **Mannes School of Music** 150 W. 85th (580-0210), and the **Manhattan School of Music** 122 Broadway (749-2802).

Movies

Most movies open in New York weeks before they're distributed across the country, and the response of Manhattan audiences and critics can shape a film's success or failure nationwide. **MoviePhone** (777-FILM/3456) allows you to reserve tickets for most major moviehouses and pick them up at showtime from the theater's automated ticket dispenser; you are charged the ticket price plus a small fee over the phone.

The Ziegfeld, 141 W. 54th St. (765-7600). Big-screen fanatics should definitely check out this cavernous theater, which projects first-run films onto one of the largest screens left in America. Tickets $9, children under 12 $4.50.

The Kitchen, 512 W. 19th St. (255-5793), between Tenth and Eleventh Ave. Subway: C or E to 23rd St. A world-renowned showcase for the off-beat from New York-based artists. Prices vary.

The Angelika Film Center, 18 W. Houston St. (995-2000), at Mercer St. Subway: #6 to Bleecker St. or B, D, F, Q to Broadway-Lafayette. Alternative (not quite underground) cinema on eight screens. Tickets $8, discounts for seniors and children.

Anthology Film Archives, 32 Second Ave. (505-5181), at E. 2nd St. Subway: F to Second Ave. A forum for independent filmmaking, focusing on the contemporary, off-beat, and avant-garde. "The American Narrative" series features 300 great American films. Tickets $7, students $6.

Museum of Modern Art: Roy and Niuta Titus Theaters, 11 W. 53rd St. (708-9490). The MoMA serves up an unbeatable diet of great films daily in its two lower-level theaters. Film tickets are included in the price of admission and are available upon request. Also ask about screenings in the video gallery on the third floor.

Sports

While most cities would be content to field a major-league team in each big-time sport, New York opts for the Noah's Ark approach: two baseball teams, two hockey teams, and two NFL football teams.

United States Open (718-760-6200), held in late Aug. and early Sept. at the USTA Tennis Center in Flushing Meadows, Queens. Get tickets (from $20) 3 months in advance for this event.

New York City Marathon: On the first Sun. in Nov., two million fans cheer 22,000 runners as they go from the Verrazano Bridge to Central Park's Tavern on the Green. 16,000 runners finish.

Baseball: The **New York Mets** bat at **Shea Stadium** in Queens (718-507-6387; tickets $6.50-15). The legendary but mortal **New York Yankees** play ball at **Yankee Stadium** in the Bronx (#63; C12; 718- 293-6000; tickets $12-21).

Football: The **New York Giants** and the **Jets** play across the river at **Giants Stadium** (201-935-3900), in East Rutherford, NJ. Jets tickets (from $25; cash only at the Meadowlands box office) are hard to come by; Giants tickets are nigh impossible—season ticket holders have booked them all for the next **40 years.**

Basketball: The **New York Knickerbockers** (that's "Knicks" to you) hold court at **Madison Square Garden** (#1; B5; 465-6741; tickets from $15).

Hockey: The mighty **New York Rangers** call **Madison Square Garden** (465-6741 or 308-6977) home; the **New York Islanders** hang their skates at the **Nassau Coliseum** (516-794-9300), Uniondale, Long Island. Tickets from $12 and $19, respectively.

MUSEUMS AND GALLERIES

For museum and gallery listings consult the following publications: *The New Yorker* (the most accurate and extensive listing), *Time Out: New York, New York,* the Friday *New York Times* (in the Weekend section), the *Quarterly Calendar,* (available free at any visitors bureau), and *Gallery Guide,* found in local galleries. Most museums and all galleries close on Mondays, and are jam-packed on the weekends. Many museums require a "donation" in place of an admission fee—you can give less than the suggested amount—and most are free one weeknight. Call ahead to confirm.

Metropolitan Museum of Art (#46; B9; 879-5500), Fifth Ave. at 82nd St. Subway: 4, 5, 6 to 86th St. If you see only one, see this. The largest in the Western Hemisphere, the Met's art collection encompasses 3.3 million works from almost every period through Impressionism; particularly strong in Egyptian and non-Western sculpture and European painting. Contemplate the sublime in the secluded Japanese Rock Garden. When blockbuster exhibits tour the world they usually stop at the Met—get tickets in advance through Ticketron. Open Sun. and Tues.-Thurs. 9:30am-5:15pm, Fri.-Sat. 9:30am-8:45pm. Donation $8, students and seniors $4.

Museum of Modern Art (MoMA), 11 W. 53rd St. (#45; B7; 708-9400), off Fifth Ave. in Midtown. Subway: E or F to Fifth Ave./53rd St. One of the most extensive contemporary (post-Impressionist) collections in the world, founded in 1929 by scholar Alfred Barr in response to the Met's reluctance to embrace modern art. Cesar Pelli's structural glass additions flood the masterpieces with natural light. See Monet's sublime *Water Lily* room, and many Picassos. Gorgeous sculpture garden. Open Sat.-Tues. 10:30am-6pm, Thurs.-Fri. noon-8:30pm. $9.50, students and seniors $6.50, under 16 free. Films require free tickets in advance. Pay-what-you-wish Fri. 4:30-8:30pm.

The Frick Collection (#50; B8), 1 E. 70th St. (288-0700), at Fifth Ave. Subway: #6 to 68th St. industrial baron Henry Clay Frick left his house and art collection to the city, and the museum retains the elegance of his French "Classic Eclectic" château. Impressive grounds. The Living Hall displays 17th-century furniture, Persian rugs, and paintings by El Greco, Rembrandt, Velázquez, and Titian. Relax in a courtyard inhabited by elegant statues surrounding the garden pool and fountain. Open Tues.-Sat. 10am-6pm Sun. 1-6pm. $5, students and seniors $3. Ages under 10 not allowed, under 16 must be accompanied by an adult.

Solomon R. Guggenheim Museum (#51; B9), 1071 Fifth Ave and 88th St. (423-3500). Many have called this controversial construction a giant turnip, Frank Lloyd Wright's joke on the Big Apple. The museum closed from 1990-92 while a ten-story "tower gallery" sprouted behind the original structure, allowing the museum to show more of its rich permanent collection of mostly 20th-century art. Open Sun.-Wed. 10am-6pm, Fri.-Sat. 10am-8pm $7, students and seniors $4, under 12 free. Pay-what-you-wish Fri 6-8pm. A $15 Two-day pass is available to this museum and **Guggenheim Museum SoHo** (#22; C3), 575 Broadway (423-3500) at Prince St. Open Sun. and Wed.-Fri. 11am-6pm, Sat. 11am-8pm. $8, students and seniors $5, and children under 12 free.

American Museum of Natural History (#38; B9; 769-5100) Central Park West, at 79th to 81st St. Subway: B or C to 81st St The largest science museum in the world, in a suitably imposing structure. Newly reopened dinosaur exhibit is worth the lines you'll inevitably face. Open Sun.-Thurs. 10am-5:45pm, Fri.-Sat. 10am-8:45pm. Donation $8, students and seniors $6, children under 12 $4. The museum also houses an **Imax** (769-5650) cinematic extravaganza on a 4-story screen. $8, students and seniors $6, children $4, Fri.-Sat. double features $7.50, children $4.

Whitney Museum of American Art (#58; C8), 945 Madison Ave. (570-3676), at 75th St. Subway: #6 to 77th St. Futuristic fortress featuring the largest collection of 20th-century American art in the world, with works by Hopper, de Kooning, Warhol, and Basquiat. Much of the Whitney's fame derives from its over-hyped Biennial exhibitions that claim to capture the pulse of American art. Open Wed. and Fri.-Sun. 11am-6pm, and Thurs. 1-8pm. $8, students and seniors $6, under 12 free. Thurs. 6-8pm free.

Cooper-Hewitt Museum (#53; B9), 2 E. 91st St. (860-6868), at Fifth Ave. Subway: #4, 5 or 6 to 86th St. Andrew Carnegie's majestic, Georgian mansion now houses the Smithsonian Institution's National Museum of Design. The playful special exhibits focus on such topics as doghouses and the history of the pop-up book. Open Tues. 10am-9pm, Wed.-Sat. 10am-5pm, Sun. noon-5pm. $3, students and seniors $1.50, under 12 free. Free Tues. 5-9pm.

American Craft Museum (#44; B7), 40 W. 53rd St. (956-3535), across from MoMA. Subway: E or F to Fifth Ave.-53rd St. Offering more than quilts, this museum revises the notion of crafts with its modern media, including metal and plastic. Open Tues.-Wed. and Fri.-Sun. 10am-6pm, Thurs. 10am-8pm. $5, students and seniors $2.50.

The Cloisters (#67; E15; 923-3700), Fort Tryon Park, upper Manhattan. Subway: A through Harlem to 190th St.; or take the M4 bus that departs from the Met. This monastery, built from pieces of 12th- and 13th-century French and Spanish cloisters, was assembled in 1938 as a setting for the Met's medieval art collection. Highlights include the Unicorn Tapestries, the Cuxa Cloister, and the Treasury, with 15th-century playing cards. Museum tours Tues.-Fri. 3pm, Sun. noon, in winter Wed. 3pm. Open Tues.-Sun. 9:30am-5:15pm. Donation $8, students and seniors $4 (includes same-day admission to Metropolitan Museum of Art).

New Museum of Contemporary Art (#44; B7), 583 Broadway (219-1222), between Prince and Houston St. Subway: N or R to Prince, or B, D, F or Q to Broadway/Lafayette. Dedicated to roles "art" plays in "society," the New Museum supports the newest and the most controversial. Many works deal with politics of identity—sexual, racial, and ethnic. Open Wed.-Fri. and Sun. noon-6pm, Sat. noon-8pm. $4, artists, seniors, and students $3, children under 12 free. Sat. 6-8pm free.

International Center of Photography (#55; B9), 1130 Fifth Ave. (860-1777), at 94th St. Subway: #6 to 96th St. Housed in a landmark townhouse built in 1914 for New Republic founder Willard Straight. The foremost exhibitor of photography in the city, and a gathering-place for its practitioners. Historical, thematic, contemporary, and experimental works, running from fine art to photojournalism. **Midtown branch** (#7; B6) at 1133 Sixth Ave. (768-4680), at 43rd St. Both open Tues. 11am-8pm, Wed.-Sun. 11am-6pm. $4, students and seniors $2.50.

Jacques Marchais Center of Tibetan Art, 338 Lighthouse Ave. (718-987-3500), Staten Island. Take bus S74 from Staten Island Ferry to Lighthouse Ave., turn right and walk up the hill. One of the finest Tibetan collections in the West. Exuding serenity, the center replicates a Tibetan temple set amid sculpture gardens. Open May-Nov. Wed.-Sun. 1-5pm. Dec.-April call ahead to schedule a visiting time. $3, seniors $2.50, children $1.

Museum of Television and Radio (#44; B7), 25 W. 52nd St. (621-6600), between Fifth and Sixth Ave. Subway: B, D, F, Q to Rockefeller Center, or E, F to 53rd St. TV memorabilia, as well as over 60,000 programs in the museum's permanent collection. With admission you can see or hear anything from the *Twilight Zone* to *Saturday Night Live.* Open Tues.-Wed. and Fri.-Sun. noon-6pm, Thurs. noon-8pm. $6, students $4, seniors and children under 13 $3.

Intrepid Sea-Air-Space Museum (#32; A7), Pier 86 (245-0072), at 46th St. and Twelfth Ave. Bus: M42 or M50 to W. 46th St. One ticket admits you to the veteran World War II and Vietnam War aircraft carrier *Intrepid,* the Vietnam War destroyer *Edson,* and the only publicly displayed guided-missile submarine, *Growler.* A breathtaking wide-screen flick puts the viewer on a flight deck as jets take off and land. Open daily 10am-5pm; Oct. 1-Apr. 30 Wed.-Sun. 10am-5pm. $10, seniors and students $7.50, ages 6-11 $5.

The Jewish Museum (#54; B9), 1109 Fifth Ave. (423-3200), at 92nd St. Subway: #6 to 96th St. Over 14,000 works detail the Jewish experience throughout history. Open Sun.-Mon. and Wed.-Thurs. 11am-5:45pm, Tues. 11am-9pm. $7, students and seniors $5, under 12 free; Tues. pay-what-you-wish after 5pm.

El Museo del Barrio (#57; B10), 1230 Fifth Ave. (831-7272), at 105th St. Subway: #6 to 103rd St. El Museo del Barrio is the only museum in the U.S. devoted exclusively to the art and culture of Puerto Rico and Latin America. Open Wed.-Sun. 11am-5pm, May-Sept. Wed. and Fri.-Sun. 9am-5pm, Thurs. noon-7pm. Suggested contribution $4, students and seniors $2.

The Museum for African Art (#22; C3), 593 Broadway (966-1313), between Houston and Prince St. in SoHo. Subway: N or R to Prince and Broadway. The museum recently expanded to feature two major exhibits a year along with smaller exhibitions of stunning African and African-American art from ancient to contemporary. Open Tues.-Fri. 10am-5:30pm, Sat.-Sun. noon-6pm. $5, students and seniors $2.50.

Museum of the City of New York (#56; B10; 534-1672), 103rd St. and Fifth Ave. next door to El Museo del Barrio. Subway: #6 to 103rd St. This museum details the Big Apple's history from the 16th century to the present through historical paintings, Currier and Ives prints, period rooms and artifacts. Open Wed.-Sat. 10am-5pm, Sun. 1-5pm. Contribution requested.

SIGHTS

You can tell tourists in New York City a mile away by a single feature—they are looking up. While the internationally famous New York skyline can be seen miles away, the tallest skyscraper seems like just another building when you're standing next to it. This sight-seeing quandary may explain why many New Yorkers have never visited some of the major sights in their hometown. In this densely packed city, even the most mind-boggling landmarks serve as backdrops for everyday life.

Lower Manhattan

Many of the city's superlatives congregate at the southern tip of Manhattan. The **Wall Street** area is the densest in all New York; Wall Street itself is less than a ½-mile long. This narrow state of affairs has driven the neighborhood into the air, creating one of the highest concentrations of skyscrapers in the world. Visit during the work week, when suspendered and high-heeled natives brandishing *Wall Street Journals* rush around between deals. After hours, these titans of trade loosen ties and suck in the ocean breeze (and a few drinks) at the mallish **South Street Seaport.** Meanwhile, around **City Hall,** the aura of 19th-century New York (bulldozed out of existence elsewhere) still predominates.

Battery Park, named for a battery of guns that the British stored there from 1683 to 1687, is now a chaotic chunk of green forming the southernmost toenail of Manhattan Island. On weekends the park is often mobbed with people on their way to the Liberty and Ellis Island **ferries,** which depart from here.

Wall Street (#21; C1-C2), once the northern border of the New Amsterdam settlement, takes its name from the wall built in 1653 to shield the Dutch colony from a British invasion. By the early 19th century, it had already become the financial capital of the United States.

Federal Hall (#24; C2), at Wall and Broad St. (825-6888). This was the original City Hall, where the 1735 trial of John Peter Zenger helped to establish freedom of the press. The steps boast an over-size statue of a tightly pantalooned George Washington on its steps (several historians have commented on the heft of Washington's rump).

New York Stock Exchange (#21; C1-C2), on the southwestern corner of Wall and Broad St. (656-5168). The Stock Exchange was first created as a marketplace for handling the $80 million in U.S. bonds that were issued in 1789 and 1790 to pay Revolutionary War debts. Arrive early in the morning, preferably before 9am, because tickets usually run out by around 1pm. The real draw is the observation gallery that overlooks the exchange's zoo-like main trading floor. Open to the public Mon.-Fri. 9am-4pm.

Trinity Church, (#14; B2-C2; 602-0872) around the corner from the NYSE, at the end of Wall St. Its seemingly ancient Gothic spire was the tallest structure in the city when first erected in 1846. The vaulted interior feels positively medieval. The church's 2½-acre yard dates from 1681.

World Trade Center (#9; B2), at Liberty Park, off Trinity Pl. Bosom companions at 110 stories each, the sleekly striped shafts (constructed in 1973) dwarf every other building in the city. They provide 10 million sq. ft. of office space for their creator, the Port Authority of New York and New Jersey. The bombing of the complex in 1993 has left no visible scars other than the ubiquitous "All visitors must carry ID" signs. Two World Trade Center has an observation deck, the **Top of the World** (323-2340), on the 107th floor. Open daily June-Sept. 9:30am-11:30pm, Oct.-May 9:30am-9:30pm. $10, seniors $8, children 6-12 $ 5.

City Hall (#23; C2) and **City Hall Park,** between Broadway, Park Row, and Chambers St. The Colonial chateau-style structure, completed in 1811, is the focus of the city's administration. City Hall Park has been a public space since 1686—home to an almshouse, a jail, a public-execution ground, and a barracks for British soldiers. On July 9, 1776, George Washington and his troops encamped on the park to hear the Declaration of Independence. Today the grounds are prettily landscaped with colorful gardens and a fountain.

Woolworth Building (#16; C2), 233 Broadway, off the southern tip of the City Hall Park. This towering commercial edifice is one of the most sublime and ornate commercial buildings in the world. Erected in 1913 to house the offices of F.W. Woolworth's corner-store empire, it stood as the world's tallest until the Chrysler Building opened in 1930. The lobby of this five-and-dime Versailles is littered with Gothic arches and flourishes, including a caricature of Woolworth himself counting change.

St. Paul's Chapel, (#15; C2; 602-0773) south of the Woolworth Building at Broadway and Fulton St. St. Paul's is Manhattan's oldest public building in continuous use. Gaze at the green churchyard and the surprising shades of the interior—baby blue, soft pink, and cream, with gold highlights. You can see George Washington's pew, where the first President worshipped on Inauguration Day, April 30, 1789. Chapel open Mon.-Fri. 9am-3pm, Sun. 7am-3pm.

South Street Seaport (#29; C2): South St., around the area of Fulton St. New York's shipping industry thrived here for most of the 19th century. Recent "revitalization" has turned the historic district, in all its fishy and foul-smelling glory, into the ritzy South Street Seaport complex, with an 18th-century market, galleries, seafaring schooners, and **Pier 16,** a shopping mall and food court. After 5pm, masses of crisply attired professionals—sneakers lurking under their skirts and ties trailing over their shoulders—flee their offices and converge here for much-anticipated cocktails.

Fulton Fish Market: at the east end of Fulton St., on South St. on the other side of the overpass. The largest (and maybe smelliest) fresh fish mart in the country. Those who can stomach wriggling scaly things might enjoy the behind-the-scenes tours of the market given some Thurs. mornings June-Oct. (market opens at 4am).

The Statue of Liberty and Ellis Island

Given by the French in 1886 as a sign of goodwill, the **Statue of Liberty** (#2; B1) has welcomed millions of immigrants to both America and the entrance to New York Harbor. Today, the statue welcomes tourists galore, as everyone and their sixteen cousins make the ferry voyage to Liberty Island. The **American Museum of Immigration** (#3; B1) resides beneath the green lady's bathrobe.

During its heroic period (1890-1920), approximately 15 million people came through **Ellis Island,** which now houses a museum that tells the tale of many Americans' ancestors. Two **ferries** bring you to and from Liberty and Ellis islands. One runs Manhattan-Liberty-Ellis, and the other Liberty State Park/Jersey City-Ellis-Liberty. Both run daily every 30min., 9:15am-4:30pm. (Ferry info 269-5755. $7, seniors $5, children 3-17 $3.)

Little Italy and Chinatown

Little Italy, a touristy pocket of Naples and Sicily nestled in the lower spine of Manhattan, is roughly bounded by Houston St. to the north, Canal St. to the south, the Bowery to the east, and Broadway to the west. The Little Italy experience revolves primarily around food. A walk up **Mulberry Street** will have you ducking under the umbrellas of sidewalk cafes. Dotted with stores selling low-cost electronics and plastics, **Canal Street** divides Little Italy and Chinatown.

New York's **Chinatown** has seven Chinese newspapers, over 300 garment factories, innumerable food shops, and houses the largest Asian community in the U.S. outside San Francisco. Vaguely bounded by Worth St. and Canal St. to the south and north, and Broadway and the Bowery to the west and east, Chinatown spills out further into the surrounding streets every year, especially to the north and east Mott Street and Pell Street are full of commercial activity, as is East Broadway.

SoHo and TriBeCa

SoHo ("South of HOW-ston Street"), bounded by Houston St., Canal, Lafayette, and Sullivan St, has become the high-priced home of New York's artistic community. Here, **galleries** reign supreme, and many established artists live and thrive on the energy of SoHo's image-intensive bars, boutiques, and restaurants. The architecture here is American Industrial (1860-1890), notable for its cast-iron facades. **Greene Street** offers the best examples. SoHo is a great place for star-gazing, too, so bring your autograph book and a bright flash for your camera. Celebrities like that.

TriBeCa ("Triangle Below Canal St."), the area bounded by Chambers St., Broadway, Canal St., and the West Side Highway, seems much more akin to the rest of the city, but the SoHo style is spreading. Today Robert DeNiro owns a grille and a film company in the neighborhood, and rents are rising. But check out the cast-iron edifices lining White St., Thomas St., and Broadway, the 19th-century buildings on Harrison Street, and the shops, galleries, and bars on Church and Reade Streets.

East Village and Alphabet City

The East Village, a comparatively new creation, was carved out of the Bowery and the Lower East Side as rents in the West Village soared and its residents sought accommodations elsewhere. A fun stretch of Broadway marks the western boundary of the East Village, although it is now very touristy. For the most part, though, the population shift has recaptured much of the gritty feel of the old Village, with older Eastern European immigrants living alongside newer Hispanic and Asian arrivals. East Village residents embody the alternative spectrum, with punks, hippies, ravers, rastas, guppies, goths, beatniks, and virtually every other imaginable group coexisting amidst myriad cafes, bars, clubs, shops, and theaters.

St. Mark's Place, running from Third Avenue at 8th Street down to Tompkins Square Park, is the geographical and spiritual center of the East Village. In the 1960s, the street was full of pot-smoking flower children waiting for the next concert at the Electric Circus. Today a Gap store sells its color-me-matching combos across the street from a shop stocking "You Make Me Sick" T-shirts.

Alphabet City lies east of First Ave., south of 14th St., and north of Houston. Here, the avenues run out of numbers and take on letters. Alphabet City is generally safe during the day, and the addictive nightlife on Avenue A ensures some protection there, but try to avoid straying east of Avenue B at night.

Cooper Union Foundation Building, 41 Cooper Sq. (353-4199). Constructed in 1859 to house the Cooper Union for the Advancement of Science and Art, a tuition-free technical and design school founded by the self-educated industrialist Peter Cooper. Cooper Union was the first college intended for the underprivileged and the first college to offer free adult-education classes.

St. Mark's-in-the-Bowery Church, 131 E. 10th St. (674-6377). The church was built in 1799, on the site of a chapel that was on the estate of Peter Stuyvesant, the much-reviled last Dutch governor of the colony of New Amsterdam. He lies buried in the small cobblestone graveyard here.

Second Avenue Deli, 156 Second Ave. (677-0606), at 10th St. This famous Jewish landmark is all that remains of the "Yiddish Rialto," the stretch of Second Ave. between Houston and 14th St. that comprised the Yiddish theater district in the early part of this century. The Stars of David embedded in the sidewalk in front of the restaurant contain the names of some of the great actors and actresses who spent their lives entertaining the poor Jewish immigrants of the city.

New York Marble Cemeteries, Second Ave. between 2nd and 3rd St., and 2nd St. just east of Second Ave. The city's first two non-sectarian graveyards. Gaze through the fences at the dilapidated tombstones. Many prominent New Yorkers have been buried here, including (at the 2nd St. yard) the improbably named Preserved Fish, a prominent merchant.

Tompkins Square Park, E. 7th St. and Ave. A. A few years ago, police officers set off a riot when they attempted to forcibly evict from the park a band of the homeless and their supporters. The park has just reopened after a two-year hiatus, and still serves as a psycho-geographical epicenter for many a churlish misfit. In 1997, several 5-foot-tall marijuana plants were found growing in the park. They were promptly uprooted once this was brought to the attention of city officials.

Lower East Side

South of Houston and east of the Bowery, in the somewhat deserted Lower East Side, you can still find some excellent kosher delis and a few old-timers who remember the time when the Second Ave. El ran. Two million Jews arrived on the Lower East Side in the 20 years before World War I. Today the Lower East Side continues to be a neighborhood of immigrants, now mostly Asian and Hispanic. But despite the population shift, remnants of the Jewish ghetto still remain. **East Broadway** epitomizes the Lower East Side's flux of cultures, with Buddhist prayer centers next to (mostly boarded up) Jewish religious supply stores, and the offices of several Jewish civic organizations. The area around Orchard and Delancey Streets, meanwhile, is one of Manhattan's bargain shopping centers.

Congregation Anshe Chesed, 172-176 Norfolk St., off Stanton St. New York's oldest synagogue now houses a small art gallery.

Beth Hamedrash Hagadol Synagogue, 60 Norfolk St. between Grand and Broome St. The best-preserved of the Lower East Side houses of worship.

Lower East Side Tenement Museum (#30; C3), 97 Orchard St. (431-0233), between Broome and Delancey St. A preserved tenement house of the type that proliferated in this neighborhood in the early part of the century. Buy tickets at 90 Orchard St. at the corner of Broome St. for a slide shows, video, and guided tour ($7, students and seniors $6). The museum gallery at 90 Orchard St. offers free exhibits and photographs documenting Jewish life on the Lower East Side (open Tues.-Sun. 11am-5pm). Tours Tues.-Fri. 1, 2, and 3pm., Sat.-Sun. every 45min. between 11am-4:15pm.

Greenwich Village

In "The Village," bordered by 14th St. to the north and Houston to the south, bohemian cool meets New York neurosis, resulting in the "downtown" approach to life. Residents with various pierced body parts share the street with NYU business students and wealthy urbanites eager to be confused with struggling artists. In contrast to the orderly, skyscraper-encrusted streets of Midtown, the Village's narrow thoroughfares meander haphazardly without regard to any underlying grid or sense of numerical order. "Greenwich Village" refers to the West Village and the rest of the area west of Broadway, including Washington Square Park and its environs. The **Christopher St.** neighborhood (Subway: #1 or 9 to Christopher St./Sheridan Sq.) is home to a vibrant (and upscale) gay and lesbian scene. A few street signs refer to Christopher St. as "Stonewall Place," alluding to the **Stonewall Inn,** the club where police raids in 1969 prompted riots that sparked the U.S. gay rights movement. **Eight Street,** from Broadway to Sixth Ave., is an anti-mall for alternateens.

The Village stays lively all day and most of the night, with an eclectic summer street life and excellent nightlife. Those seeking propriety should head uptown immediately. Everyone else should revel in the funky atmosphere, stores, and people-watching.

Washington Square Park (#13; B4), between University Pl. and MacDougal St., and Waverly Pl. and W. 4th St. The universally acknowledged heart of the Village since the district's days as a suburb. Subway: A, B, C, D, E, F, or Q to W. 4th St./Washington Sq. In the late 1970s and early 80s, Washington Square Park became a base for low-level drug dealers, and a rough residential scene. The mid-80s saw a noisy clean-up campaign that has allowed a more diverse cast of characters to return. Today musicians play, misunderstood teenagers congregate, dealers mutter cryptic words, homeless people try to sleep, pigeons strut, and children romp in the playground. The fountain in the center of the park provides an amphitheater for entertainers of widely varying degrees of talent.

Washington Memorial Arch, at the north end of Washington Square Park. The Arch, which marks the end of Fifth Ave., was built in 1889 to mark the centennial of Washington's inauguration as President. The statues on top depict multi-talented George in poses of war and peace. The arch is actually hollow—every year the NYU band opens the door at the base and trudges up the 110 stairs to *Pomp and Circumstance* to kick off the NYU commencement in the Park.

New York University (313; B4). The country's largest private university has dispersed its buildings and eccentric students throughout the Village. One of the city's biggest landowners (along with the city government, the Catholic Church, and Columbia University), NYU is noteable for its hip students, its takeover of historic buildings, and some of the most amazingly ugly architecture in the Village. Many buildings around Washington Square are proudly festooned with the purple NYU flag. **NYU Information** is located at 70 Washington Sq. South., at the southeast corner of the park.

Church of the Ascension, at the corner of 10th St. and Fifth Ave. A fine 1841 Gothic church with a notable altar and stained-glass windows. Former President John Tyler eloped with his second wife here in 1844. Open daily noon-2pm and 5-7pm.

The Salmagundi Club, 11th St. and Fifth Ave. New York's oldest club for artists. Founded in 1870, the club's building is the one of the only clubhouses left from the area's heyday at the pinnacle of New York society. Open 1-5pm daily. Call 255-7740 for details.

Forbes Magazine Galleries, 12th St. and Fifth Ave. (206-5548). Malcolm Forbes's vast and eccentric collection of random *stuff.* Open Tues.-Sat. 10am-4pm. Free.

Forbidden Planet, 821 Broadway (473-1576), at 12th St. New and used comic books, D&D figurines, a whole section of V.C. Andrews books, and a shelf about serial killers at this large sci-fi/fantasy warehouse. Unhealthily thin boys and the death-goth girls who love them shop here. Open daily 10am-8:30pm.

Strand, 828 Broadway (473-1452), at 12th St. New York's biggest and most-loved used-book store. A must-see. 8 mi. of shelf space holding nearly 2 million books. Staffers will search out obscure titles at your bidding. Ask to see a catalog, or better yet, get lost in the shelves on your own. The best of the best. Open Mon.-Sat. 9:30am-9:30pm, Sun. 11am-9:30pm.

Grace Church, 800 Broadway, between 10th and 11th. Constructed in 1845, gothic Grace Church used to be *the* place for weddings. The dark interior has a distinctly Medieval feel. Open Mon-Thurs. 10am-5pm, Fri. 10am-4pm, Sat. noon-4pm.

Other Music, 15 E. 4th St. (477-8150) between Broadway and Lafayette. Specializing in the alternative and avant-garde, from Stereolab to recordings of feedback. Pricey obscure stuff abounds, but there is a sizeable used CD section. Posters and flyers keep the clientele updated on where to see performers who push the boundaries of music. Open Mon.-Sat. noon-9pm, Sun. noon-7pm.

Balducci's, 422 Sixth Ave. at W. 8th St. The legendary Italian grocery has grown over the years from a sidewalk stand to a gourmand's paradise. Marvel at its orgy of cheese barrels, bread loaves, and chilled vegetables, and get into a staring contest with the live, bug-eyed lobsters (hint: they'll win).

Jefferson Market Library, 425 Sixth Ave. (243-4334), at W. 10th St. Built as a courthouse in 1874, the library is a landmark Gothic structure complete with detailed brickwork, stained-glass windows, and a turreted clocktower. Inside, the original pre-Raphaelite stained glass graces the spiral staircase. The brick-columned basement now serves as the Reference Room. Open Mon. and Thurs. 10am-6pm, Tues. noon-6pm, Wed. noon-8pm, Sat. 10am-5pm.

Lower Midtown and Chelsea

Neither coldly commercial nor hot 'n' trendy, lower Midtown, like the third little bear's bowl of porridge, seems just right. Neoclassical architecture and generous avenues create an aura of refinement. At the 23rd St.-Madison Square intersection, for example, four of the earliest skyscrapers form a sub-skyline, one of the city's overlooked visual treasures.

Home to some of the most fashionable clubs, bars, restaurants, and galleries in the city, **Chelsea** has lately witnessed something of a rebirth. A large and visible gay and lesbian community and an increasing artsy-yuppie population have given Chelsea, which lies west of Fifth Ave. between 14th and 30th St., the flavor of a lower-rent West Village.

Madison Square Park, at 27th St.—the end of Madison Ave. The park, opened in 1847, originally served as a public cemetery. Check out the statues of your favorite Civil War generals. Since developers have only just started to sink their cranes into this area, a number of the landmark buildings from years past remain. The area near the park sparkles with funky architectural gems.

Flatiron Building (#12; B5), at the intersection of Broadway, Fifth Ave., 22nd St., and 23rd St. (off the southwest corner of Madison Square Park). Yet another member of the "I-used-to-be-the-world's-tallest-building" club, the Flatiron is often considered the world's first skyscraper. Originally called the Fuller Building, the photogenic wedge shape earned it its current nickname. St. Martin's Press, publisher of such titles as *Let's Go Map Guide: New York City*, occupies roughly half the building's space.

Gramercy Park, at the foot of Lexington Ave. between 20th and 21st St., In 1831, developer and plant-lover Samuel B. Ruggles drained an old marsh and laid out 66 building lots around the periphery of the central space. Buyers of his lots received keys to the private park which for many years were made of solid gold. The park, with its wide gravel paths, remains the only private park in New York, immaculately kept by its owners.

Hotel Chelsea, 222 W. 23rd St. between Seventh and Eighth Ave. This historic Hotel has sheltered many a suicidal artist, most famously Sid Vicious of the Sex Pistols. Edie Sedgwick made pit stops here between Warhol films and asylums before lighting the place on fire with a cigarette. Countless writers, memorialized by the plaques outside, spent their final days searching for inspiration and mail in the lobby. Arthur Miller, Vladimir Nabokov, and Dylan Thomas all made use of the hotel.

Hip, New Galleries, on W. 22nd between Tenth and Eleventh Ave. The galleries clustered here are hotter and more adventurous than those in SoHo. Check out the Dia Center for the Arts (548 W. 22nd, 989-5912; $4, students and seniors $2), Max Protech (511 W. 22nd, 633-6999), and D'Amelio Terras (525 W. 22nd, 352-9460).

East Midtown and Fifth Avenue

East of Sixth Ave., from about 34th St. to 59th St., lies the bulk of East Midtown. This is the land of fast-talking, high-stakes business deals, where it always seems dark because the buildings are so tall. East Midtown gives New York its most common stereotypes—businesswomen in Ann Taylor suits and white Keds, flamboyant skyscrapers, chic boutiques, and rude cabbies. Don't let it all frighten you; let yourself be swept away in the frenzy.

Empire State Building, (#10; B5; 736-3100), Fifth Ave. between 33rd and 34th St. The Empire State remains New York's best-known and best-loved landmark, and dominates the postcards, the movies, and the skyline. The limestone and granite structure, with glistening mullions of stainless steel, stretches 1454 ft. into the sky; its 73 elevators run on 2 mi. of shafts. The nighttime view will leave you gasping. Although it is no longer the tallest building in the U.S., or even in New York (stood up by the twin towers of the World Trade Center), in Midtown it towers in relative solitude, away from the forest of monoliths that has grown around Wall St. $6, children under 12 and seniors $2.25; observatory open daily 9:30am-midnight, tickets sold until 11:30pm.

Pierpont Morgan Library (#17; C6), 29 E. 36th St. (685-0610). Subway: #6 to 33rd St. Come to this Renaissance-style *palazzo* to see the book raised to the status of a full-fledged fetish object in a stunning collection of rare books, sculpture, and paintings gathered by the banker and his son, J.P. Morgan, Jr. Open Tues.-Fri.10:30am-5pm, Sun. noom-6pm. Suggested contribution $5, students and seniors $3. Free tours Tues.-Fri. 2:30pm.

New York Public Library, (#11; B6; 661-7220) Fifth Ave. between 40th and 42nd St., near Bryant Park. On sunny afternoons, throngs of people perch on the marble steps, which are dutifully guarded by the mighty lions Patience and Fortitude. This is the world's seventh-largest research library; witness the immense third-floor reading room. Free tours Tues.-Sat. at 11am and 2pm. Open Mon. and Thurs.-Sat. 10am-6pm, Tues.-Wed. 11am-7:30pm.

Bryant Park spreads out soothingly against the back of the library along 42nd St. to Sixth Ave. Site of the World's Fair in 1853, in the afternoon people of all descriptions crowd into the large, grassy, tree-rimmed expanse to talk, relax, and sunbathe. The stage that sits at the head of the park's big, grassy field plays host to a variety of free cultural events throughout the summer, including screenings of classic films, jazz concerts, and live comedy. Call 397-8222 for an up-to-date schedule of events.

Grand Central Terminal (#18; C6), east of Bryant Park along 42nd St., where Park Ave. would be between Madison and Lexington Ave. The great transportation hub where almost all dazed tourists got their first glimpse of the glorious city. The massive Beaux Arts front, with the famed 13ft. clock, gives way to the Main Concourse, a huge lobby area which becomes zebra-striped by the sun falling through the slatted windows. Constellations are depicted on the sweeping, arched expanse of green ceiling.

Chrysler Building (#27; C6), 42nd St. and Lexington. The New York skyline would be incomplete without the Chrysler's familiar Art Deco headdress. The structure was built by William Van Allen as a series of rectangular boxes and topped by a spire modeled on a radiator grille. During construction, the Chrysler building engaged in a race with the Bank of Manhattan building for the title of the world's tallest structure. Work on the bank was stopped when it seemed as if it had already won. The devious Chrysler machinists then brought out and strapped on the spire, which had been secretly assembled inside. So when completed in 1929, this elegantly seductive building stood as the world's tallest. The Empire State Building topped it a year later.

United Nations Building, (#31; C6; 963-4475), First Ave. between 42nd and 48th St. Feel like leaving the country? The UN is actually *not* located in New York City; its grounds are international territory and thus not subject to the laws and jurisdiction of the U.S. Outside, a multicultural rose garden and a statuary park provide a lovely view of the East River. Inside, go through security check and work your way to the back of the lobby for the informative tours of the **General Assembly.** Tours about 45min., leaving every 15min. from 9:15am to 4:45pm daily, available in 20 languages. $7.50, seniors over 60 and students $5.50, under 16 $3.50. **Visitor's entrance** at First Ave. and 46th St. You must take the tour to get past the lobby. Sometimes free tickets can be obtained when the U.N. is in session (Oct.-May); call 963-1234.

Rockefeller Center (#42; B7), between 48th and 51st St. and Fifth and Sixth Ave. A monument to the conjunction of business and art, Rockefeller Center is the world's largest privately owned business and entertainment complex, occupying 22 acres of midtown Manhattan. On Fifth Ave., between 49th and 50th St., the famous gold-leaf statue of Prometheus sprawls out on a ledge of the sunken **Tower Plaza** while jet streams of water pulse around it. The Plaza serves as an overpriced open-air cafe in the spring and summer and as an ice-skating rink in the winter. The **stores** on Fifth Ave. from Rockefeller Center to Central Park are the ritziest and most expensive in the city.

The RCA Building rises to 70 stories at Sixth Ave., and remains the most accomplished artistic creation in the Rockefeller Center complex. Every chair in the building sits less than 28 feet from natural light. Nothing quite matches watching a sunset from the 65th floor as a coral burnish fills the room. The **NBC Television Network** makes its headquarters here, allowing you to take a behind-the-scenes look at their operations. Currently opens three shows to guests: *Saturday Night Live, Late Night with Conan O'Brien,* and *Rosie O'Donnell.* Call 664-4444 for general info. Tours run every 15min. Mon.-Sat. 9:15am-5pm; $10.

Radio City Music Hall, (#42; B7; 632-4041) at the corner of Sixth Ave. and 51st St. Despite its illustrious history and wealth of Art Deco treasures, Radio City was almost demolished in 1979 to make way for new office high-rises. However, the public rallied and the hall was declared a national landmark. First opened in 1932, the 5874-seat theater remains the largest in the world. The brainchild of Roxy Rothafel, it was originally intended as a variety showcase. Instead, the hall functioned primarily as a movie theater; over 650 feature films debuted here from 1933 to 1979, including *King Kong, Breakfast at Tiffany's,* and *Doctor Zhivago.* The Rockettes, Radio City's chorus line, dance on. Tours of hall are given every 30min. daily 10am-5pm. $12, children under 7 $6.

Seagram Building (#60; C7), 375 Park Ave., between 52nd and 53rd St. Ludwig Mies Van der Rohe's dark and gracious creation is pure skyscraper, with no frills or silly froufrou like the buildings near Grand Central—a paragon of the austere International Style. Van der Rohe envisioned its plaza, with its two great fountains, as an oasis from the tight canyon of skyscrapers on Park Ave.

F.A.O. Schwarz, 767 Fifth Ave. (644-9400), at 58th St. Reclaim that inner brat, or just take in the opulence of one of the world's largest toystores, including complex Lego constructions, environmentally responsible toys, life-sized stuffed animals, and a separate annex exclusively for Barbie dolls. Open Mon.-Sat. 10am-7pm, Sun. 11am-6pm.

Plaza Hotel, Fifth Ave. and 59th St., at the southeast corner of Central Park. The legendary Plaza was built in 1907, at the then-astronomical cost of $12.5 million. Its 18-story, 800-room French Renaissance interior flaunts five marble staircases, countless ludicrously named suites, and a two-story Grand Ballroom, the site of many of New York's finest proms. Past guests and residents have included Frank Lloyd Wright, the Beatles, F. Scott Fitzgerald, and, James Brown. *Let's Go* recommends the $15,000-per-night suite.

West Midtown

Decidedly more grimy than its eastern counterpart, the area west of Sixth Ave. between 31st and 59th St. shines in a more neon, less gold-foiled way, with Broadway theaters, countless hotels, and peep shows all beckoning through the grime. **Times Square** still smoulders at the once-seedy core of the Big Apple (now being cleansed by Disney), while the nearby **Theater District** stretches from 41st to 57th St. along Broadway, Eighth Ave., and the streets that connect them. If you want to see the city of *Midnight Cowboy,* where Broadway lights splash on the dingy canvas of old warehouses and steamy streets, shuffle through the west side.

Pennsylvania Station (#1; B5), 33rd St. and Seventh Ave. One of the less engrossing pieces of architecture in West Midtown, Penn station, as a major subway stop and train terminal, can at least claim to be highly functional. (Subway: #1, 2, 3, 9, A, C, or E to 34th St./Penn Station). The original Penn Station, a classical marble building modeled on the Roman Baths of Caracalla, was demolished in the 60s. The railway tracks were then covered with the equally uninspiring **Madison Square Garden** complex (see **Sports** p. 13).

James A. Farley Building, 421 Eighth Ave., facing the Garden. New York's immense main post office luxuriates in its 10001 ZIP code. A swath of Corinthian columns shoulders broadly across the front, and a 280-ft. frieze on top of the broad portico bears the bold, Cliff Clavenesque-motto of the U.S. Postal Service: "Neither snow nor rain nor heat nor gloom of night stays these couriers from the swift completion of their appointed rounds."

Macy's (#6; B6), 34th St. (695-4400), between Seventh Ave. and Broadway. With nine floors (plus a lower level) and some two million sq. ft. of merchandise, monolithic Macy's has come a long way from its beginnings in 1857, when it grossed $11.06 on its first day of business. The store sponsors the **Macy's Thanksgiving Day Parade,** a New York tradition buoyed by helium-filled 10-story Snoopies and Barnies, as well as marching bands, floats, and general hoopla. Open Mon.-Sat. 10am-8:30pm, Sun. 11am-7pm. Subway: #1, 2, 3, or 9 to Penn Station, or B, D, F, N, Q, or R to 34th St.

Times Square (#4; B6), a.k.a. the intersection of 42nd St. and Broadway. Look for the flickering lights. Times Square has worked hard to improve its image, and Disney's planned entertainment megaplex will hasten the gentrification. Robberies are down by 40%, pick-pocketing and purse-snatching by 43%, and the number of area porn shops has plummeted by more than 100 from its late-70s climax of 140. Still, Times Square is Times Square. Teens coninue to roam about in search of fake IDs, hustlers are as eager as ever to scam suckers, and every New Year's Eve, millions booze and schmooze under the pretense of watching an electronic ball drop. One-and-a-half million people pass through Times Square every day, as do lots of subway lines (#1, 2, 3, 7, and 9, and A, C, E, N, R, and S).

Carnegie Hall, 57th St. and Seventh Ave. (247-7800). How do you get to Carnegie Hall? Practice, practice, practice. This venerable institution was founded in 1891 and remains New York's foremost soundstage. Tchaikovsky, Caruso, Toscanini, and Bernstein have played Carnegie; as have the Beatles and the Rolling Stones. Other notable events from Carnegie's playlist include the world premiere of Dvořák's *Symphony No. 9 (From the New World)* on December 16, 1893, and an energetic lecture by Albert Einstein in 1934. Tours are given Mon., Tues., Thurs., and Fri. at 11:30am, 2, and 3pm ($6, students and seniors $5). Carnegie Hall's free **museum** displays memorabilia from its illustrious century of existence (open daily 11am-4:30pm).

Upper East Side

The Upper East Side, land of decadence, drips with money the length of Central Park. The Golden Age of the East Side society epic began in the 1860s and progressed until the outbreak of World War I. Scores of wealthy people moved into the area and refused to budge, even during the Great Depression when armies of the unemployed pitched their tents across the way in Central Park. These days, parades, millionaires, and unbearably slow buses share Fifth Avenue. **Madison Avenue** graces New York with luxurious boutiques and most of the country's advertising agencies. Fifth Ave. in the 80s and 90s becomes **Museum Mile,** which includes the Metropolitan, the Guggenheim, the ICP, the Cooper-Hewitt, and the Jewish Museum, among others (see **Museums and Galleries,** p. 14).

Bloomingdale's sits in regal splendor at 1000 Third Ave. (705-2000), at E. 59th St. Watch the eternal tango between casual shoppers and perfume spritzers on the first floor, and dodge the throngs of tourists buying up the Clinique counter.

Gracie Mansion (#65; C9), between 84th and 90th St. along East End Ave., at the northern end of Carl Schurz Park. The residence of every New York mayor since Fiorello LaGuardia moved in during World War II. Now Rudy Giuliani occupies this hottest of hot seats. To make a reservation for a tour, call 570-4751. Tours Wed.; suggested donation $3, seniors $2.

Temple Emanu-El, (744-1400) at the corner of Fifth Ave. and 65th St. The temple's name means "God is with us"; it's the largest synagogue in the U.S. Outside, Eastern details speckle the limestone and otherwise Romanesque structure. Inside, the nave bears Byzantine-style ornaments and seats 2500 worshippers—more than St. Patrick's Cathedral. Open daily 10am-5pm.

Metropolitan Museum of Art, 1000 Fifth Ave., near 82nd St. Fountains and sore-footed museum-goers flank its majestic presence. The largest in the Western hemisphere, the Met's art collection encompasses some 33 million works (see **Museums and Galleries,** p. 14).

Central Park

Central Park's 843 acres—which contain lakes, ponds, fountains, skating rinks, ball fields, tennis courts, a castle, an outdoor theater, a bandshell, and two zoos—may be roughly divided between north and south at the main reservoir. The southern section affords more intimate settings, serene lakes, and graceful promenades, while the northern end has a few ragged edges. The small metal four-digit plaques bolted to the lampposts tell you where you are; the first two digits tell you what street you're nearest (e.g., 89), and the second two whether you're on the east or west side of the Park (even numbers mean east, an odd west). In an emergency, use one of the many call-boxes located throughout the park.

Central Park Zoo, (#47; B8; 861-6030), Fifth Ave. at 64th St. Roving herds of sugar-hyped children make even the drowsy reptiles tremble in fear, while the monkeys effortlessly ape their visitors. $2.50, seniors $1.25, children 3-12 50¢. Open April-Oct. Mon.-Fri. 10am-5pm, Sat.-Sun. 10:30am-5:30pm; Nov.-March daily 10am-4:30pm.

Central Park Reception Center, (794-6564) now housed in the Dairy building of the Central Park Zoo. Pick up the free map of Central Park and the seasonal list of events. Open Tues.-Thurs. and Sat.-Sun. 11am-5pm, Fri. 1-5pm; Nov.-Feb. Tues.-Thurs. and Sat.-Sun. 11am-4pm, Fri. 1-4pm.

Wollman Skating Rink, (396-1010) just west of the zoo. Ice- or roller-skating $4, children under 12 and seniors $3, plus $6.50 skate or rollerblade rental. Open summer daily 11am-6pm; winter Sat.-Sun only. A nice addition to the roller rink is the railed ledge overlooking it, from which an unparalleled view of midtown can be had free of charge.

Friedsam Memorial Carousel, (879-0244) 65th St. west of Center Dr. The 58-horsepower carousel was brought from Coney Island and fully restored in 1983. Open daily 10am-6:30pm, weather permitting. Thanksgiving to mid-March Sat.-Sun. 10:30am-4:30pm. 90¢.

Sheep Meadow, directly north of the Carousel from about 66th to 69th St., on the western side of the Park. This is the largest chunk of greensward, exemplifying the pastoral ideals of the Park's designers and today's teenage crowds. Sheep did graze here until 1934, but after that the Park could afford lawn mowers and so terminated the flock. Inside "The Meadow," legions of the young and beautiful (and their friends) play frisbee and drink beer. It is not uncommon to join a stranger's game, but ask first. Directly north of the meadow, the crowd instantly ages about 50 years.

The Lake, in the western half of the park from about 72nd St. to 77th St., is still a dramatic sight in the heart of the City. The 1954 **Loeb Boathouse** (517-2233) supplies all necessary romantic nautical equipment. Its mighty rental fleet includes rowboats, swanboats, and even gondolas. Open daily April-Sept. 10:30am-4:30pm, weather permitting. Rowboats rented for $10 per hr., plus $30 deposit. Bike rental also available; call 861-4137 for info.

Strawberry Fields, west of the Lake at 72nd St. and West Dr. Sculpted as Yoko Ono's memorial to John Lennon, the fields are located directly across from the Dakota Apartments where Lennon was assassinated and where Ono still lives. Picnickers and 161 varieties of plants now inhabit the rolling hills around the star-shaped "Imagine" mosaic on sunny spring days. On John Lennon's birthday on October 9th, in one of the largest unofficial Park events, thousands gather here to remember—or as time passes, to "imagine"—what the legend was really like.

Swedish Cottage Marionette Theater, (988-9093) at the base of Vista Rock near the 79th St. Transverse. Regular puppet shows June to mid-August. Shows Mon.-Fri. 10:30am and noon. $5, children $4. Reservations required.

Delacorte Theater, up the hill from the Cottage Theater. This round wooden space hosts the wildly popular **Shakespeare in the Park** series each midsummer. These plays often feature celebrities and are always free. Come early: the theater seats only 1936 lucky souls (see **Theater,** p. 11).

Great Lawn, north of the Theater. Often the site of large concerts. Paul Simon sang here, the Stonewall 25 marchers rallied here, and the New York Philharmonic and the Metropolitan Opera Company frequently give free summer performances here. Unless something is going on, the Lawn tends to be a bit forlorn.

Upper West Side

Along Central Park West the well-to-do residents can look down at doormen or across the park to their soul mates on the Upper East Side. Further west, plenty of the antique stores, clothing emporiums, and fern-colored singles bars attest to the comfortable West-Siders' tastes, but the white-collar takeover that began in the 1950s with the construction of Lincoln Center hasn't wiped out all the ethnic enclaves. **Columbus Avenue** is great for people-watching and moderately-priced eats, and leads up to the Museum of Natural History (see **Museums and Galleries,** p. 14). **Broadway,** the most colorful street on the West Side, is crammed with delis, theaters, and boutiques. On the sidewalk desperate hawkers peddle everything from bun dumplings to worn copies of *Juggs* magazine to the kitchenware of yesteryear. From Midtown, Broadway leads uptown to **Columbus Circle,** 59th St. and Broadway, the symbolic entrance to the Upper West Side and the end of Midtown—with a statue of Christopher himself.

Zabar's, 2245 Broadway (787-2000), at 81st St. Wander down the tempting aisles of the gourmet food market that never ends.

Lincoln Center, Columbus Ave. between 62nd and 66th St. (LINCOLN/546-2656). The seven facilities that constitute Lincoln Center, the cultural hub of the city, accommodate over 13,000 spectators at a time. They are Avery Fisher Hall, the New York State Theater, the Metropolitan Opera House, the Library and Museum of Performing Arts, the Vivian Beaumont Theater, The Walter Reade Theater, and the Juilliard School of Music. At night, the Metropolitan Opera House lights up, making its chandeliers and huge Chagall murals visible through its glass-panel facade.

American Museum of Natural History, Central Park West between 78th and 81st St. Built in 1899 by J.C. Cady and Co. and since added to, the museum looks as unwieldy as a prehistoric mastodon. The museum's patron saint Teddy Roosevelt is honored at the main entrance on Central Park West by a triumphal arch and a racist bronze (see **Museums and Galleries,** p. 14).

Harlem

The first blacks to live in Harlem were the slaves of Dutch settlers; it took an enormous influx of rural Southerners during and after World War I to create the Harlem known today as one of the capitals of the black Western world. On the East Side above 96th St. lies **Spanish Harlem,** known as El Barrio ("the neighborhood"), and on the West

Side lies Harlem proper, stretching from 110th to 155th St. West of Morningside Ave. and south of 125th St. is the Columbia University area, known more commonly as **Morningside Heights** than as a part of Harlem. **125th Street,** also known as Martin Luther King Jr. Boulevard, spans the heart of traditional Harlem with fast-food joints, jazz bars, and the Apollo Theater (at 253 W. 125th St.; see **Entertainment and Nightlife,** p. 8). All these neighborhoods heat up with street activity, not always wholesome; visit Harlem during the day or go there with someone who knows the area.

Columbia University (#33; A11), between Morningside Dr. and Broadway, 114th and 120th St. New York's Ivy Leaguer, chartered in 1754, is now co-ed and also has cross-registration across the street with all-female **Barnard College.** Columbia's urban campus occupies the former location of the Bloomingdale Insane Asylum. Call 854-2854 to schedule a tour.

Cathedral of St. John the Divine (#35; B11), along Amsterdam Ave. (316-7540) between 110th and 113th St. promises to be the world's largest cathedral when finished. Construction, begun in 1812, will not be completed for perhaps another century or two. Open daily 7am-5pm; admission $1, students and seniors 50¢.

Riverside Church, near Columbia at 120th St. and Riverside Dr. The observation deck in the tower commands an amazing view of the bells within and the expanse of the Hudson River and Riverside Park below. Open Mon.-Sat. 9am-4:30pm, admission $1; Sun. service 10:45am. Free church tours given Sun. 12:30pm.

Grant's Tomb, diagonally across Riverside Dr. from Riverside Church (666-1640). Once a popular monument, the mausoleum now attracts only a few brave souls journeying to see the sarcophagous of Grant and his wife Julia. Open daily 9am-5pm. Free.

Masjid Malcolm Shabazz, 102 W. 116th St. (662-2200), at Lenox Ave. Malcolm X was once a minister beneath this silver dome. Visit Fri. at 1pm and Sun. at 10am for services and information.

Brooklyn

Brooklyn is Dutch for "Broken Land," and the name fits—the city's most populous borough is an aggressively heterogenous terrain, where ultra-orthodox *Hasidim* rub elbows with black teenagers on a street covered with signs *en español.* Ethnic and religious groups don't always get along, but an indominable pride in their home unites them. What goes on in Brooklyn tends to happen on the streets and out of doors, whether it's neighborhood banter, baseball games in the park, ethnic festivals, or pride marches. The Dutch settled the borough in the 17th century. When asked to join New York in 1833, Brooklyn refused, saying that the two cities shared no interests except common waterways. Not until 1898 did Brooklyn decide, in a close vote, to become a borough of New York City.

The Brooklyn Bridge spans the East River from lower Manhattan to Brooklyn. Built in 1883, the bridge was one of the greatest engineering feats of the 19th century. Today you too can take the mile-long stroll, along with companies of ambitious commuters in Reeboks. Look straight up at the cables and Gothic arches and watch the sun weaving through the constantly shifting steel cobweb above. Walk on the left side of the pedestrian path; the right is reserved for bicycles. A ramp across from City Hall begins the journey from Manhattan (subway: #4, 5, or 6 to Brooklyn Bridge).

Brooklyn Promenade: Head south on Henry St. after the Brooklyn Bridge, then turn right on Clark St. toward the river for a gorgeous view of Manhattan. Many prize-winning photographs have been taken from this point overlooking the southern tip of Manhattan and New York Harbor.

Brooklyn Heights, just west of Cadman Plaza Park and south of Old Fulton St. Subway: M or R to Borough Hall. Once George Washington's headquarters during the Battle of Long Island, now-posh Brooklyn Heights has atttracted many authors, from Walt Whitman to Norman Mailer, with its beautiful old brownstones, tree-lined streets, and proximity to Manhattan. In 1965, Brooklyn Heights became New York's—and the nation's—first Historic District. Today the brownstones of the 19th-century house the young, upwardly mobile set and a diverse collection of families.

Atlantic Avenue, just south of Brooklyn Heights, is home to a large Arab community, with second-hand stores and inexpensive Middle Eastern bakeries and grocery stores. Atlantic runs from the river to Flatbush Ave. At the Flatbush Ave. Extension, pick up the **Fulton Street** pedestrian mall.

Williamsburg, several blocks north of downtown Brooklyn (subway: J, M, or Z to Marcy Ave.), has a strong Hasidic Jewish and Polish population alongside more recent Hispanic immigrants. The quarter encloses Broadway, Bedford, and Union Avenues. Recently, Manhattanite artists have been drawn to Williamburg for its cheap loft spaces, and a funky, lo-fi crop of hip restaurants and shops has followed close behind (subway: L to Bedford Ave.).

Park Slope, bounded by Flatbush Ave., 15th St., Fifth Ave., and Prospect Park, the area has a high level of ethnic diversity and tolerance due to its academic, professional residents. Dreadlocked blacks strolling arm-in-arm with fashion model blondes are as common as same-sex couples kissing out in the open (earning its nickname "Dyke Slope"). Subway: F to Seventh Ave.

Prospect Park, (718-965-8951) off Flatbush Ave. Subway: #2 or 3. At the north corner of the park stands **Grand Army Plaza,** an island in the midst of the borough's busiest thoroughfares. The park's largest open area is the sweeping, 90-acre **Long Meadow,** the longest open urban parkland in North America.

Brooklyn Museum, (718-638-5000) off Eastern Pkwy. at Washngton Ave. Subway: #2 or 3 to Eastern Pkwy. The mammoth "little" sibling of the Met, with a huge permanent collection and a monumental neoclassical exterior. Check out the outstanding Ancient Greek, Roman, Middle Eastern, and Egyptian galleries on the 3rd floor; gems from Sargent and the Hudson River School shine in the American Collection on the 5th floor. Open Wed.-Fri. 10am-5pm, Sat. 10am-9pm, Sun. 11am-6pm. Suggested donation $4, students $2, seniors $1.50, children under 12 free.

Botanic Gardens, (718-622-4433), next to the museum at 1000 Washington Ave. Subway: #2 or 3 to Eastern Pkwy. This 52-acre fairy land was founded in 1910 on a reclaimed waste dump. Throughout the secluded park are several stunning theme gardens. Open April-Sept. Tues.-Fri. 8am-6pm, Sat.-Sun. and holidays 10am-6pm; Oct.-March Tues.-Fri. 8am-4:30pm, Sat.-Sun. and holidays 10am-4:30pm. $3, students and seniors $1.50, children 5-15 50¢. Free Tues.

Sheepshead Bay, on the southern edge of Brooklyn. Subway: D or Q to Sheepshead Bay. The name applies to both a body of water (really part of the Atlantic) and a mass of land, and refers to a fish that has since abandoned its native waters for the cleaner Atlantic. Emmons Avenue runs along the bay and faces **Manhattan Beach,** a wealthy residential section of doctors and mafioso just east of Brighton Beach.

Brighton Beach, just south and west of Sheepshead Bay. Subway: D or Q to Brighton Beach. Nicknamed "Little Odessa by the Sea," Brighton Beach has been home to Russian emigrés since the turn of the century. In late June and early July, old Eastern Europeans complaining about their bodily ailments, Spandex-clad girls listening to Top 40 music on their Walkmans, and middle-aged couples drowning sunburns in Noxzema are all wowed by the Blue Angels air shows.

Coney Island, west of Brighton Beach. (Subway: B, D, F, or N to Stillwell Ave. Once a resort for the City's elite, made accessible to the rest of the Apple because of the subway, the fading park still warrants a visit. The **Boardwalk,** once one of the most seductive of Brooklyn's charms, now squeaks nostalgically as tourists are jostled by roughnecks. Enjoy a hot dog and crinkle-cut fries at historic **Nathan's,** Surf and Sitwell.

The Cyclone, 834 Surf Ave. (718-266-3434), at W. 10th St. Built in 1927, Coney Island's Cyclone remains the most terrifying roller coaster ride in the world. Enter its 100-second-long screaming battle over nine hills of rickety wooden tracks—the ride's well worth $4. Open daily mid-June to Labor Day noon-midnight; Easter weekend to mid-June Fri.-Sun. noon-midnight.

New York Aquarium, (718-265-3474) Surf and West 8th, on Coney Island. Go meet a walrus, dolphin, sea lion, shark, or other ocean critter in the aquarium's tanks. The first beluga whale born in captivity was raised here. Watch a solitary scuba diver be immersed in a tank full of feeding sharks. Open daily 10am-5pm, holidays and summer weekends 10am-7pm; $7.75, children 2-12 and seniors $3.50.

Queens

In this urban suburbia, the American melting pot bubbles away with a more than 30% foreign-born population. Immigrants from Korea, China, India, and the West Indies rapidly sort themselves out into neighborhoods where they try to maintain the memory of their homeland while living "the American Dream."

Queens is easily New York's largest borough, covering over a third of the city's total area. If you visit only one of its neighborhoods, let it be **Flushing.** Here you will find some of the most important colonial neighborhood landmarks, a bustling downtown, and the largest rose garden in the Northeast. (Subway: #7 to Main St., Flushing.) Nearby **Flushing Meadows-Corona Park** was the site of the 1964-1965 World's Fair, and now holds Shea Stadium.

Astoria/Long Island City, the northwest region of Queens, just across the East River from Manhattan. Subway: N to Broadway and 31st. Long Island City, spliced with subway lines and covered in grime, has long been Queens's industrial powerhouse. In the 1930s, Newtown Creek saw as much freight traffic as the Mississippi River. The area has lately acquired a reputation as a low-rent artists' community, though it remains to be seen whether the avant-garde will cross the river. Astoria, known as the "Athens of New York," has by some estimates the second-largest Greek community in the world. The area is also home to a sizable Italian community.

Ridgewood, southeast of Long Island City, was founded by Eastern European and German immigrants a century ago. More than 2000 of the distinctively European, attached brick homes here receive protection as landmarks, securing Ridgewood's listing in the National Register of Historic Places, but the adjacent Brooklyn ghetto of Bushwick has frayed the neighborhood's edges.

Queens Botanical Garden, (718-886-3800) 5 blocks down Main St. toward Corona Park from the #7 subway station in Flushing. Queens' regal plant shrine boasts a 5000-bush rose garden (the largest in the northeast), a 23-acre arboretum, and more than nine acres of "theme gardens." Open mid-April to mid-Oct. Mon.-Fri. 8am-6pm, Sat.-Sun. 10am-7pm; mid-Oct. to mid-April Tues.-Sun. 9am-4:30pm. Suggested donation $1, children 50¢.

The Bronx

While the media presents "Da Bronx" as a crime-ravaged husk, the borough offers its few tourists over 2000 acres of parkland, a great zoo, turn-of-the-century riverfront mansions, and thriving ethnic neighborhoods, including a Little Italy to shame its counterpart to the south. But if you're not heading for Yankee Stadium, stay out of the South Bronx unless you're with someone who knows the area.

Bronx Zoo: The most obvious reason to come to the Bronx. The largest urban zoo in the United States, it houses over 4000 animals. Soar into the air for a funky cool view of the zoo from the

Skyfari aerial tramway that runs between Wild Asia and the Children's Zoo ($2). The **Bengali Express Monorail** glides 'round Wild Asia (20 min.; $2). If you find the pace too hurried, saddle up a camel in the Wild Asia area ($3). Call 718-220-5142 three weeks in advance to reserve a place on a **walking tour.** Pamphlets containing self-guided tours are available at the Zoo Center for 75¢. Parts of the zoo close down during the winter (Nov.-April); call 718-367-1010 or 718-220-5100 for more info. Open Mon.-Fri. 10am-5pm, Sat.-Sun. 10am-5:30pm; Nov.-March. daily 10am-4:30pm. Free Wed., otherwise $6.75, seniors and children $3. For disabled access, call 718-220-5188. Subway: #2 or 5 to E. Tremont Ave.-West Farms Sq. and walk 4 blocks north up Boston Rd. to the Zoo entrance.

New York Botanical Garden, (718-817-8705) north across East Fordham Rd. from the zoo. Snatches of forest and virgin waterways allow you to imagine the area's original landscape. Garden grounds open Tues.-Sun. 10am-6pm. $3, seniors, students, and children $1. Free Wed. Subway: #4 or D to Bedford Park Blvd. and walk (or take the Bx26, 12, 19, or 41 bus) 8 blocks east.

Wave Hill, 675 W. 252nd St. (718-549-3200), in Riverdale. An estate that was home to Samuel Clemens (Mark Twain), Arturo Toscanini, and Teddy Roosevelt (not simultaneously). The estate currently offers concerts and dance amidst its greenhouses and spectacular formal gardens. Picnic in the world-famous gardens with an astonishing view of the Hudson River. Gardens open June to mid-Oct. Tues.-Thurs. and Sat.-Sun. 9am-5:30pm, Fri. 9:30am-dusk; mid-Oct. through May Wed.-Sun. 10am-4:30pm. Tues. free. Sat.-Sun. $4, seniors and students $2.

Van Cortlandt Park, (718-430-1890) in the northwest corner of the borough. The city's third-largest jolly green giant spreads across 1146 acres of ridges and valleys. The slightly grungy park contains golf courses, tennis courts, baseball diamonds, soccer, football, and cricket fields, kiddie recreation areas, a large swimming pool, and a lake teeming with bemused fish.

Staten Island

Getting there is half the fun. The free (!) 30min. ferry ride from Manhattan's Battery Park to Staten Island is as unforgettable as it is inexpensive. Or, you can drive from Brooklyn over the **Verrazano-Narrows Bridge,** the world's second-longest (4260ft.) suspension span. In recent years Staten Islanders have unsuccessfully lobbied to have Staten Island declared an independent municipality. For tourists, the sights on the island cluster around the beautiful 19th-century **Snug Harbor Cultural Center,** at 1000 Richmond Terrace (take the S40 bus from the ferry terminal).

Newhouse Center for Contemporary Art: A small gallery displaying American art with an indoor/outdoor sculpture show in the summer. Open Wed.-Sun. noon-5pm; suggested donation $2.

Staten Island Children's Museum: (718-273-2060). Funky interactive exhibits for the five- to 12-year-old in you. Open July-mid-Sept. Tues.-Sun. 11am-5pm, Thurs. 11am-7pm; mid-Sept.-July Tues.-Sun. noon-5pm. $4.

Staten Island Botanical Gardens: (718-273-8200). Beds of lilies, lilacs, sunflowers, and snapdragons—and a Butterfly Garden. Open daily dawn-dusk; tours available by appointment.

ACCOMMODATIONS

Hotels

Carlton Arms Hotel, 160 E. 25th St. (679-0680), between Lexington and Third Ave. Subway: #6 to 23rd St. Each room was designed by a different avant-garde artist. Singles around $54; doubles around $68, with bath around $76. Triples with bath around $91. Pay for 7 nights up front and get a 10% discount.

Make summer reservations at least 2 months in advance, and call to confirm 10 days in advance. Student and foreigner discounts.

Portland Square Hotel, 132 W. 47th St. (382-0600 or 800-388-8988; fax 382-0684), between Sixth and Seventh Ave. Subway: B, D, F, or Q to 50th St.-Sixth Ave. Rooms are carpeted, clean, and comfy. Perks include A/C, cable TV, and a safe in every room, but the hotel's main asset is its location. Singles with shared bath $50, with private bath $75; doubles $94; triples $109; quads $114.

Herald Square Hotel, 19 W. 31st St. (279-4017 or 800-727-1888, fax 643-9208; email hersquhtl@aol.com), at Fifth Ave. Subway: B, D, F, N, or R to 34th St. In the original home of *Life* magazine. Works by some of America's best illustrators adorns the lobby, halls, and rooms. Tiny, clean, rooms with color TV, small refrigerators, phones, and A/C. Singles with shared bath $50, with private bath $75; doubles $95, with 2 beds $105. International students get a 10% discount. Reservations recommended.

Pioneer Hotel, 341 Broome St. (226-1482; fax 266-3525), between Elizabeth St. and the Bowery. Located between Little Italy and the Lower East Side in a century-old building, the Pioneer is a good, no-frills place to stay if you want to be close to the addictive nightlife of SoHo and the East Village. All rooms have TVs and sinks. Ceiling fans alleviate the need for A/C. Generally tight security at night in a neighborhood that requires it. Singles $36, $226 per week; doubles $55, with bath $65; triples $80, with bath $88. Reservations recommended.

Pickwick Arms Hotel, 230 E. 51st St. (355-0300 or 800-PICKWIK/742-5945; fax 755-5029), between Second and Third Ave. Subway: #6 to 51st St. or E, F to Lexington-Third Ave. Business types congregate in this well-priced, mid-sized hotel. Chandeliered marble lobby filled with the soothing sounds of Top-40 Muzak contrasts with tiny rooms and microscopic hall bathrooms. Roof garden and airport service available. Check-in 2pm, check-out 1pm. A/C and TV in all rooms. Singles $50-85 (some with bath); doubles with bath $105-115. Double bed with sofa $125. Additional person in room $15. Gets very busy, so make reservations.

Hostels

Gershwin Hotel, 7 E. 27th St. (545-8000; fax 684-5546; email gershwin@attmail.com; http://www.netprop.com/gershwin), between Fifth and Madison Ave. Subway: #6, N, or R to 28th St. With a large, cool building full of pop art, pop art furniture, and artsy twenty-somethings, the Gershwin seems more like an MTV show than a place to stay. It hosts a next-door gallery, an amateur band night (Sat.), and a hip bar, all of which throw frequent parties. Summer days in the rooftop garden often become unabashed scamming sessions. Passport or ID proving out-of-state or foreign residence required. 21-day max. stay. 24hr. reception. Check-out 11am. No curfew. 4-bed dorms $22 per bed, tax included. Private rooms available. Doubles and triples $75-120.

New York International HI-AYH Hostel, 891 Amsterdam Ave. (932-2300; fax 932-2574), at W. 103rd St. Subway: #1, 9, B, or C to 103rd St. Kitchens and dining rooms, laundry machines ($1), TV lounges, and an outdoor garden. Walking tours and outings. Individual lockers. 7-night max. stay in summer. Open 24hr. Check-in any time, check-out 11am (late check-out fee $5). No curfew. Members $27 per night in summer, $14 in off-season, nonmembers $10, $17. Complimentary linen. Wheelchair access.

Street Index

33

List of Sights